Acknowledge

G000017949

I am indebted to Julia Sallabank who initiated and steered me through the early stages of this revised edition, and to Bruce Wade who edited the manuscript so skilfully in the final stages.

I should also like to thank my own students who have been willing to update and work on a few projects which were devised before they were even born!

However, my greatest debt of gratitude lies with the countless teachers who shared with me their experience of doing project work in their own countries: Argentina, Belgium, Finland, France, Greece, Hong Kong, Italy, Norway, Poland, Portugal, Serbia, Spain, Switzerland, and Turkey. It is their enthusiasm and contribution to the workshops, seminars, lectures, and talks on project work which have made this second edition possible.

I should also like to acknowledge and thank the following teachers who submitted projects:

Algeria: Habib Safi

Argentina: Alicia Artusi

Australia: Margaret Herbert, Nicholas Cope, Jonathan Crichton, Clare Kitada

Brazil: Sonia Regina Limn, Neide Ferreira Gaspar, Eliane Prado Marcondes, Rosana Prado, Julia Casarin

Czech Republic: Dagmar Pivodova, Eva Zimova, Jarmila Cernoskova, Jirina Riedlova

Greece: Marina Mattheoudakis

Hong Kong: Sue Fitzgerald, Chi-Wai Lok

Italy: Manuela Reguzzoni, Maria Bassi, Joanna Pearson

Japan: Duane Kindt

Myanmar: U Than Pe

Poland: David Lear

Portugal: Joao Manuel Banha Correia

Slovakia: Antonia Pifkova

Spain: Roser Costa, Albert López-Guindal

Thailand: Teeranart Teepapal, Virachak Sangvong, Wayne Rimmer

Turkey: Charlotte Samli, Clem McDonnell

Ukraine: Larisa Shishkina

UK: Tom Le Seelleur, George Kershaw, Yvonne Howe, Lili Wilson, Fionnuala O'Connell, Sheila Longman

For Xanthé and Dominic – for always being there and for their constant support.

Contents

The author and series editor

Diana L. Fried-Booth began her teaching career in London before moving to Ghana where she taught English Language and Literature, returning to take up a research post in Rural Communications at Reading University. She went on to work in the West Midlands on language resource centres in primary schools and an integration scheme for immigrants in the secondary sector. She worked for the Bell Educational Trust for 8 years, where she was involved with teacher training and directing pre-sessional courses for various universities. As a freelance teacher trainer she has worked on short courses for The British Council worldwide. For many years she has been closely involved with the Cambridge Examinations in English and currently holds a number of posts in both the Lower (KET, PET) and Upper Main suite (FCE, CAE, CPE) examinations. She has written many ELT books, one of which, *Focus on Preliminary English Test,* won the English Speaking Union's Duke of Edinburgh Prize for Course Books for Adult Learners. She is co-founder of TEFLIS, a professional organization for teachers in the south-west of England, where she continues to teach part-time.

Alan Maley worked for The British Council from 1962 to 1988, serving as English Language Officer in Yugoslavia, Ghana, Italy, France, and China, and as Regional Representative in South India (Madras). From 1988 to 1993 he was Director-General of the Bell Educational Trust, Cambridge. From 1993 to 1998 he was Senior Fellow in the Department of English Language and Literature of the National University of Singapore. He is currently a freelance consultant and Director of the graduate programme at Assumption University, Bangkok. Among his publications are *Literature,* in this series, *Beyond Words, Sounds Interesting, Sounds Intriguing, Words, Variations on a Theme,* and *Drama Techniques in Language Learning* (all with Alan Duff), *The Mind's Eye* (with Françoise Grellet and Alan Duff), *Learning to Listen* and *Poem into Poem* (with Sandra Moulding), *Short and Sweet,* and *The English Teacher's Voice.*

Foreword

Project Work was the very first title to be published in the Resource Books for Teachers series back in 1986. The fact that it is still in print, 15 years later, testifies to the value teachers have found in this kind of work.

However, many things have changed since 1986. *Project Work* was a pioneering effort to interest teachers in carrying out projects. Since then, project work has gained wide acceptance, and teachers have experimented with it in a wide variety of teaching environments worldwide. Furthermore, the advent and rapid spread of the Internet has vastly facilitated access to information which has made project work more feasible in non-English-speaking contexts.

The new edition of *Project Work*, completely rewritten, reflects these changes. The projects it contains have been contributed by teachers in many different places, most of them non-English speaking countries. All these projects have been designed and tried out by teachers in their own schools. There is also a wider variety of project types, ranging from those which can be done in the classroom to more ambitious ones out in the real world.

Project Work offered a powerful methodology for involving students in an authentic learning experience with language used for genuine communication purposes. It was student-centred, and it resulted in a tangible end-product. All these features continue to operate. For teachers looking for ways to 'get real' in the teaching of English, these 34 new projects are a rich resource.

We hope that teachers will be inspired to develop their own projects—just as the contributors to this new edition did.

Alan Maley

Introduction

Who this book is for

This book is for teachers who want their students to develop confidence in using English in the real world, the world *outside* the classroom. Consciously or unconsciously, students bring the outside world into the classroom, but they may not always have the opportunity to activate what they know and use it in the outside world. Project work takes the experience of the classroom out into the world and provides an opportunity for informal learning. The potential benefit for students is clear: they are working on a topic of interest to them and using language for a specific purpose, with a particular aim in mind. What has already been learnt can now be put to use and what is needed can be learnt when it is needed.

In schools and colleges anywhere in the world you see students carrying bags and rucksacks with logos in English. Students discuss films about to be released starring English-speaking actors, buy magazines with pictures of their favourite pop groups, wear T-shirts printed with slogans and logos in English. They talk about football teams, Formula 1 racing, and international tennis championships. During their breaks they eat and drink food with recognizably English names, read English advertisements, access the Internet, listen and sing along to the latest hits. This book sets out to offer a framework for harnessing all this potential and more.

The projects included in this book have been submitted by teachers from all over the world. Since the first edition of *Project Work* there has been a steady increase in interest as teachers from different countries have taken up ideas, extended them, and turned them into projects that suited their own teaching situation. In order to compile this new edition teachers were invited to submit their projects, using a standard form describing the project and how they and their students had tackled it. It has not been possible to include all the projects, but the diversity of those included reflects the sheer range and variety of project work worldwide. Each project reflects individual teachers' unique contribution to the project work carried out by their students.

Update

The original reason for developing project work at the beginning of the 1980s resulted from the impact of the communicative approach on what teachers were doing in the classroom. Project work pushed forward the boundaries by bringing students into direct contact with authentic language and learning experiences not usually available within the four walls of an ELT classroom using textbooks.

Project work offered learners an opportunity to take a certain responsibility for their own learning, encouraging them to set their own objectives in terms of what they wanted and needed to learn. This tenet still holds true. In the light of all the contributions to this new edition and further developments in teaching methodology, the tenet is even more securely rooted.

Background

Since the novelty of those early experimental days when teachers sent students out to stand on street corners with their questionnaires or to interview unsuspecting foreign visitors, project work has evolved beyond recognition. What was once perceived by both teachers and students as a marginal activity to be done last thing on a Friday afternoon has now achieved international respectability. Ways had to be found to equip the learner to assume the independence that is thought to be desirable. And project work is, I believe, one of these ways.

Defining a project

Project work is student-centred and driven by the need to create an end-product. However, it is the route to achieving this end-product that makes project work so worthwhile. The route to the end-product brings opportunities for students to develop their confidence and independence and to work together in a real-world environment by collaborating on a task which they have defined for themselves and which has not been externally imposed.

Project work lends itself to many different approaches in a variety of teaching situations. It draws together students of mixed ability and creates opportunities for individuals to contribute in ways which reflect their different talents and creativity. The less linguistically-gifted student may be a talented artist, able to create brilliant artwork, thus gaining self-esteem, which would be unlikely in a more conventional language lesson. The collaborative process, relying as it does on the involvement and commitment of the individual students, is the strength of a project. There is no concrete evidence to suggest why and how project work is more or less successful with some learners. Future research into learner differences may shed light on this. What teachers do seem to agree on, however, is that even the most reluctant, skeptical learner is susceptible to peer group enthusiasm and derives benefit from taking part in a project.

The majority of projects in this book have been contributed by teachers who are not working in an English-speaking environment. This fact alone is an indication of how much things have changed in terms of accessing suitable materials, and the degree to which the process of communication has been transformed by the use of computers, the Internet, and email. It is still the case that students studying in an English-speaking environment have an advantage in being surrounded by the target language, but students' motivation and commitment is generally what drives a project forward and determines its overall success.

How to use this book

Each project has three main stages:

1 The planning stage: in conjunction with you, students discuss the scope and content of their project in English or their mother tongue. This is the stage where you and they discuss and predict their specific language needs as well as the end-product. It is usually the stage where a lot of ambitious ideas get whittled down to realistic objectives! But it is also the stage where you should be able to judge whether the idea will take off or whether it is likely to present problems, either logistically or because only a minority of students seem to be really interested.

2 The implementation stage: at this stage students carry out the tasks in order to achieve their objective. It may involve working outside the classroom or not, depending on the nature of the project. For example, interviewing someone may rely on an individual visiting the class, but the real-world element remains in the form of the visitor and their contribution. Your role during this stage is one of support and monitoring.

3 The third stage is the creation of the end-product, which will be something tangible. As the projects in this book illustrate, end-products can take many different forms—poster, wall display, magazine, news sheet, three-dimensional model, website, video film, audio recording, etc. Colleagues and other students may be invited to share in the end-product. There may also be some kind of formal or informal evaluation and feedback on what students have produced. You may wish to devise a follow-up programme to address the language needs that have come to light during the second stage.

Project framework

Level

This indicates the language-ability level recommended by the teacher who carried out the project. Nevertheless, many projects can be adapted to different levels and teachers' expectations vary, as do interpretations of words like 'intermediate' or 'elementary'. Some projects are clearly only suitable for elementary or advanced learners, but in between these two levels there is considerable scope for adapting a project if the idea appeals.

Age range

As with level, the age range has been recommended by the teacher who has experience of the project. However, as this book is aimed at teenagers and adult learners (for lower age groups see *Projects with Young Learners*, OUP), you can assume that all the projects are usable within the whole range—from young adolescent to adult.

Time

This indicates how much time a project took in one particular teaching situation. However, lesson lengths and the number of lessons available per week vary enormously from school to school, let alone country to country, so any recommendation must be regarded as flexible.

General aims

This includes both intangible aims like stimulating students' motivation as well as the end-product.

Language aims

Some projects clearly require specific language skills and these are recommended. Often a project offers the opportunity to integrate all four language skills (see page 98).

You are the person best placed to know whether a project will draw on language skills your students already possess or whether there are certain skills you need to pre-teach. If you can anticipate the need for certain skills, you can prepare in advance. Because of time constraints, when you are doing a short project you may have to respond as the project develops. If you are faced with a language difficulty or specific vocabulary relevant to the whole class, deal with it in a teacher-centred way, but not when it might interrupt the momentum of the project. In such a case, make a note of points to be followed up later.

Location

This will tell you where work on the project takes place and whether students need to leave the confines of the classroom and/or school.

Resources

Project work need not be expensive. In fact, some projects may involve no extra costs at all, but always make sure that a project falls within your budget before you consider embarking on it. Some classrooms are better equipped than others. However, some of the resources recommended may be optional. Always consider adapting a project if the idea attracts you or see whether colleagues or students can help with some of the equipment and resources.

Teacher preparation

This explains what you will need to think about and provide before the project starts. Always allow yourself plenty of time so that you avoid false starts which dampen enthusiasm and may make it difficult to resurrect the idea.

Student preparation

This explains what is required on the part of the students. It may be no more than organizing themselves into groups or it may mean that they have to collect some realia in advance. Allow a sensible time frame and check that sufficient students have complied with what was asked of them before attempting to get the project under way.

Procedure

This covers the stages of carrying out a project from introduction of the idea through to the end-product. You should be thoroughly familiar with the stages so that you can anticipate any problems, clarify your own role, and communicate this confidence to your students. However, be aware that the unpredictable nature of projects may require you to respond to events as they arise even if they are not foreseen within the outline procedure.

Follow-up

This provides suggestions for extending the project, especially the language content. If during the project you identified language areas that need more work, this is the time when you can follow up the points you noted earlier and do some

close-focus language work. You could also give students a
worksheet on a particular language point to keep for reference.

Variation

This explains how some projects can be adapted to different
levels, be given a different focus, develop different skills or
content areas, or how the basic idea or topic can be made
appropriate to different cultures and countries.

Comments

These may be based on a teacher's experience or added by the
author as additional advice or comment.

Organizing a project

Timing

For the teacher, project work offers a stimulating break from routine and invigorates the relationship with your class long after the project has finished. Judging from the number of teachers engaged in project work, the rewards clearly outweigh the demands.

Choosing when to do a long-term project needs careful consideration, whereas a short-term project probably requires a power surge! If you are finding it difficult to keep on top of all your lesson planning, preparation, and marking on a daily basis, it is not a good idea to embark on a project in addition to everything else. Why not consider a project as a means of injecting new life into students' language learning?

Timetabling

Each project recommends the time the teacher originally allocated to it. For example, *The pocket money survey* (see page 104) requires approximately six lessons, *Valentine cards* (see page 94) two hours, and *The island* (see page 101) could occupy an entire school year. Teaching circumstances vary enormously and no two classrooms are identical. But a project can be flexible. If you are attracted to a particular topic, see whether the project can be organized to fit into your students' timetable. You might be able to devote a few consecutive lessons to a project, especially if you can see a connection between the skills the project encourages and those arising in the next section of the students' coursebook. Alternatively, you might be able to allocate one lesson a week for a few weeks to a project if your students are willing to work on some aspect of the project outside the classroom. If you are teaching on a short summer-school programme or there is a slack period, possibly after examinations or towards the end of the school year, this too could be the right time.

What kind of project?

How much time you decide to spend on a project will depend on your own particular circumstances. You may want to concentrate on a project for all the English language lessons during a limited period of two or three weeks. You may see a project as only part of the overall programme, occupying one day a week—there are no hard and fast rules about it. You will also need to anticipate how you will get hold of information, although if you have access to the Internet, this obviously makes obtaining information much easier and faster than it used to be!

Once you have decided that your teaching timetable allows you to do a project, you will have to decide on the time you want to allocate to it, the scope of the project, and whether it fits into your syllabus. You will not be able to answer any of these questions definitively until students have decided what they are interested in.

Where does the initial impetus come from? It can come from you, it may come from an individual within the group, or it may arise out of the dynamics of the group, with no one clear contributing source.

Any teacher who has a close working relationship with a group and is sensitive to its needs will naturally come to learn about that group's interests. Over time, issues will be discussed and certain topics will have grabbed the students' imagination more than others. Only you can recognize these moments of creative, imaginative contact between you and your students, and it is these that provide the opportunity for exploring an issue. The most important thing is to seize the moment and capitalize on it as the focal point for an extended language activity: *a project*.

A glance through all the projects in this book reveals that there is no shortage of areas of interest from a student's point of view. The starting point is the conviction that the subject is worth pursuing and that there is a strong, corporate desire to pursue it, whether for three hours, three weeks, or three months.

Initial planning

It is no exaggeration to say that the success of a project depends very largely on how well-organized you are, and careful, detailed attention to planning the project will communicate confidence to your students. As already mentioned, you have to be alert to the potential for a project but at the same time you may envisage implementing a project at a particular stage in a course and therefore need to plan ahead rather than wait for inspiration to strike the group. In this case you have to take the initiative, to remain flexible to the students' response to the idea, and to carry out some teacher preparation behind the scenes. A long-term project which aims to make a video film, produce a booklet, wall display, or other tangible end-product will require more detailed planning than a short-term project which depends on accessing information quickly, for example, by interviewing tourists arriving at a railway station.

Storing material

Each individual project has its own requirements although not every project will necessitate a storage system. However, you need to ensure that you can at least initially provide the means and the space to store everything students collect. In all probability students will not always retrieve their own material, as other students in the class will need to refer to it, so it is essential that you encourage a system that is well-organized, easily accessible, clearly indexed, hardy, and secure. A number of simple systems will do: a cardboard box, a plastic crate with index cards on the front, or an electronically stored record of information on computer if you have IT facilities in the classroom.

Student safety

Consider carefully how much work will have to be undertaken by students outside the classroom and how much of the project will rely on obtaining formal parental permission. Some projects such as *The island* (see page 101) are classroom-based, whereas other projects like *The zoo* (see page 74) involve work outside the classroom. If you are working on short courses in a temporary situation, it is essential to establish that you and your students are covered by the school's insurance policy.

Before students are sent out to collect information, ensure the necessary arrangements are in place, unless gaining entry to a place constitutes part of the language task. The projects in this book alert you to the necessity of setting up these arrangements in advance.

If students are going to stand around at a busy station hoping to interview travellers, it is best to contact the appropriate authorities beforehand to avoid unforeseen difficulties. In some instances, of course, permission will be refused, and it is worth compiling a list of no-go areas for your own use and that of your colleagues.

Some teachers and schools issue students with identity badges bearing the school name and logo and signed by the school head/director. Students studying in an English-speaking environment should always work in pairs or small groups outside the school. On the whole, students seem to work more successfully in pairs than in small groups. In any case, unless they are very confident, they are unlikely to want to work alone. Most projects rely on pair work or small-group collaboration. Never underestimate the very real fear some students have of getting lost. Give them clear maps of the area where they will be, the numbers of buses they need to take to get to their destinations, photocopied pictures of landmarks so they recognize where they are, and so on.

Occasionally students find themselves in socially embarrassing situations and may need to extricate themselves. You cannot predict the unpredictable, but try to equip students through role-play in class to cope with potential unforeseen circumstances. For example, getting separated from their group or missing a bus may mean having to ask a stranger for help. If your students have mobile phones, ask them to keep them switched on so you can contact them if you have to, and give them numbers where they can contact you.

Students studying in their own countries are less likely to feel disorientated or to encounter socially embarrassing or linguistically problematic situations. Nevertheless, they may still have to contend with spontaneous language situations, for example, meeting a foreigner, if the target language is English. They will also need to manipulate the language with a reasonable degree of skill and confidence in order to attain their objectives. Once again, role-play in the classroom or with a colleague playing the role of a helpful or unhelpful stranger can equip students with strategies for dealing with the unexpected.

Classroom location

One major consideration when organizing project work is *where* in the school the project should be based if it is going to last more than a few lessons.

If you have your own base, you will be able to store your material quite easily. If you share a room, try to use a cupboard or a cabinet which can be locked when not in use. If you have no regular, permanent base you could use lightweight plastic or cardboard storage containers which can be safely stored in the school library or book store but which can be collected at the start of each lesson and returned at the end. A rota of students to help with this task will make life easier!

A classroom with easy access is preferable to one in the heart of the building, especially if there is a lot of coming and going which could disturb other classes. It is an advantage if the room can be adapted for entertaining visitors, showing videos, or bringing in equipment. Ideally, the classroom furniture should be mobile, so that it can be stacked away and reassembled for workshop purposes. Lighting is important, particularly if a video camera is to be used, and blackout facilities are also desirable for showing a film. Internal noise can disturb visiting speakers, and noisy discussion can disturb everyone else.

If you want to display students' work and you don't have your own space, ask colleagues whether they would be willing to let you use their classroom walls. Otherwise, consider other communal areas, such as corridors, the canteen, reception, or recreation areas.

Getting a project started

Getting a project off the ground successfully will depend on a number of factors already discussed. To begin at the end— project work culminates in a tangible end-product which can be anything from a handout to a radio programme, from a group report to a video film. In fact, during the course of a project the end-product may change considerably from what was initially envisaged. This does not matter and in any case you will only discover it with hindsight!

Assuming you and your students have agreed that a project sounds like a good idea, what next? If you have access to your own previous students' or other teachers' projects and can describe and explain what was done, this always acts as a stimulus, providing you avoid overwhelming your current students and overshadowing the topic they have in mind. The rest is really up to you and your students' enthusiasm, inspiration, and initiative. This is not intended to sound vague or unhelpful, but if you have read this far, you will have realized the open-ended nature of project work and will appreciate there is no magic formula.

Language monitor

A new topic area will quickly generate the need to acquire new language in the form of vocabulary, structures, and pronunciation. It is a good idea to have ready a way of coping with this demand.

If students can feel that they have the time and opportunity to master the use of language that either you or they have identified as being necessary for a certain stage in a project, this will go a long way to increasing their confidence and language competence.

One way to do this is to produce a language monitor which focuses on vocabulary and structures that have identified as being useful. Figure 1 gives an example of a class vocabulary

monitor. Every time students identify a gap in their vocabulary
or come across a new word or phrase that is useful, they record
it on a piece of card and pin it on a designated noticeboard.
This allows other students to read it and absorb the word or
phrase—the meaning, pronunciation, associated words or
collocations, and how to use it in a sentence. They can also add
their own cards. The vocabulary monitor remains on the
noticeboard throughout the project, constantly available for
reinforcement and consolidation. It can also be used as a source
of vocabulary games.

In addition to this or as an alternative, if you have suitable
computer facilities available, electronic lists could be created.
Students can add to the lists in the same way as the noticeboard.
The updated list can be printed out at regular intervals and put
on the noticeboard and handouts given to the students.

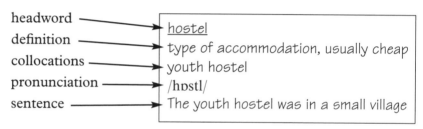

Figure 1

The project in action

Role of the teacher

Wherever you teach and in whatever circumstances, your role remains fundamentally the same—that of a participant and coordinator when necessary, responding to a language point that may need presenting or revising, and anticipating linguistic or logistical problems. In other words, you are a figure in the background evaluating and monitoring the language being used.

Your role is perhaps most vital in trying to maintain an overview and inspiring confidence so that your students feel they are learning by working towards their objectives. Whether you are involved in a project based solely in the classroom, or engaged in one which takes students outside the classroom, you will need to develop strategies for dealing with the language that arises, whether you can predict it or not.

One factor more associated with long-term projects than short-term ones is that your role will change and it is important to communicate this to your colleagues. The irony is of course that the more *passive* you appear to be, the more successful the project is in terms of student autonomy and independent learning. Passivity does not indicate inactivity. Sensitive teachers provide moral support in such a way that students hardly notice them. Simply *being* with your students, working alongside them, awaiting their next move or their return if they are undertaking something outside the classroom, and being absorbed in how they are handling their own language needs, enables you to hold the group together without overtly and busily *doing* anything.

Short-term projects

By their very nature, short-term projects are concentrated and less likely to generate unpredictable language. In this case, language monitoring is relatively straightforward, given that there are clearly defined objectives.

Some of the projects in this book suggest specific grammar or structural points that you may need to consider, but it is not desirable to be prescriptive, as each teacher is confronted with a different set of variables in any one classroom.

Long-term projects

It is not necessary to structure the overall language content at
the beginning of a long-term project. As the project gets under
way, you will become aware that some grammar which you know
your students have not covered will be coming up. Sometimes
the gaps in your students' knowledge will become evident as a
result of what they *discover* they need to know.

In a mixed-ability class you may have to individualize, use peer-
teaching strategies, or allow things to go untaught. For example,
a weak student who is enjoying the work, and perhaps showing
signs of confidence in trying to use the language, however
inaccurately, may best be overlooked rather than receive negative
attention. Teachers can usually help an individual outside project
contact time if they think it necessary.

As the project develops, you may be able to see ways of planning
ahead in order to systemize language input, or you may put the
project on hold for a lesson while you deal with a specific
language point. This will depend on your other commitments
and how much time and energy you can devote to this one
activity. One of the guiding principles is not to worry, as your
anxiety will communicate itself to your students, but to remain
positive and try to ensure that the work is enjoyed and felt to be
worthwhile.

Monitoring

Despite the argument for the non-interventionist approach for
part of the time that you and your students are working on a
project, it is still necessary to devise strategies for monitoring
what is going on in terms of language use.

Depending on the length of your project, you could consider a
review sheet (see Figure 2) which helps students consolidate
what they have covered. You could give this out at the end of a
short project, or after a few lessons or weeks during a longer
project. Obviously, you have to collect and respond to these
reviews as soon as possible. Although this is time-consuming, it
is of mutual benefit to you and the individual student.

Another strategy is for you to circulate whilst students are
working together and to make discreet notes on what students
are doing. They may be using a great deal of redundant
language, or using their mother tongue, but some of what you
hear or read may be significant and suggest further practice. You
may also want to make a note of effective use of language. The
monitoring process can then be seen as a way of rewarding or
praising students.

Weekly review

Name ....

Class ....

Dates ....

1 What new vocabulary have you learnt this week?

....

....

2 Which of these new words can you use with confidence?

....

....

3 Which of these new words do you feel unsure about?

....

....

4 What can you say/do this week that you couldn't say/do last week?

....

....

5 What have you learnt about the language that you didn't know before this week?

....

....

6 What have you read this week? ....

What have you listened to this week? ....

What have you written about this week? ....

What have you spoken about this week? ....

7 Did you use any textbooks this week? Give details.

....

....

8 What homework have you done this week?

....

....

9 Any comments?

....

....

Figure 2

The error monitor (Figure 3) is designed to be used with individual students, but can also be used with large classes. Devise your own system of symbols for error analysis, and encourage your students to practise self- or peer-correction. You can record what you consider to be the most useful errors in one column, using a symbol to indicate the error. Then the student can write in the correction, which you will then need to check. This method is greatly appreciated by students at every level because it personalizes feedback and helps them to realize their efforts are not going unnoticed.

ERROR MONITOR

Name: .... **Week 1 / Monday 24 Nov.**

Error	Correction
What means this ? Q	What does this mean ?

Figure 3

One further strategy (Figure 4) allows you to focus on whether there is a pattern in an individual student's errors by categorizing the errors. This approach may be too painstaking to use very often, but it is another way of alerting students to how they can improve their language level by being more aware, and ultimately taking more responsibility for their own learning.

Students at upper-intermediate or advanced levels can be encouraged to monitor each other using the error monitor sheets, but this kind of decision will depend on the rapport within the group. It may work for certain nationalities, but other nationalities will be reluctant, resentful, or suspicious if they know their peers are recording their mistakes, or else feel that what they consider to be the teacher's role is being neglected or usurped.

ERROR MONITOR

Name: ....

Grammar	Vocabulary	Functions	Pronunciation
~~What means X?~~	~~I'm injury.~~	Requests—~~May you help me?~~	youth— ~~/juːs/~~
What does X mean?	I'm injured/hurt.	Could you help me?	/juːθ/

Figure 4

Finally, if students are out and about, it is unlikely that you can implement any kind of systematic monitoring. You may be able to check up that all is well—that they're in the right place at the right time—but beyond that you should not attempt to intervene. Allow time for feedback in the classroom and then listen to what they say, read what they write, and talk with them about what they have been doing.

Classroom feedback sessions

If you and your students are going to exploit language points and collated information, you must ensure that you focus on what is significant and useful for everyone, otherwise students will get bored.

If a project moves very quickly, a lot of half-learnt, half-understood language items may begin to accumulate. You can set a homework task based on learning new vocabulary or you can ask students to itemize some of the language that they have come across but not understood. These items can be used as a springboard for more intensive work and possibly left till the follow-up stage of a project. With an advanced-level group, you may be able to distribute these items among the group and suggest they prepare micro-teaching slots in which they teach the rest of the class. Items can range from specific grammatical points to functions, idioms, phonological points, and even factual information that may emerge from the project content.

Some feedback sessions may turn into workshops in which your students sort out their materials, make wall displays, write up reports, download material from the Internet, prepare or design questionnaires. Your role should be one of constant participation, even though you yourself may not be directing anything specific. If occasionally there is a surfeit of printed information, try pushing desks or tables together and leaving the material there for everyone to browse through, so students feel they are not missing out on anything.

Troubleshooting

Some of the projects in this book draw attention, usually in the 'Comments' section, to problems that can occur in relation to that particular project, but there a few problems that are more general. These are listed in Figure 5.

POTENTIAL PROBLEM	SUGGESTIONS
A sense of anticlimax after initial burst of enthusiasm; students may feel overwhelmed.	Reassure and encourage. This is a natural reaction—ask a colleague to join a lesson to admire and praise what students are doing.
One or two students are reluctant to join in, or show signs of being disruptive.	Be patient and hope that team spirit or peer-group pressure will prevail; suggest a role which involves collating the data the rest of the class is collecting; suggest their responsibility is to keep a class project diary. If resources allow, this could include Polaroid shots of groups at work.
The project comes to an end prematurely and there is no end-product.	Maintain a positive attitude and present an overview of what was gained and learnt.
Relationships become fraught and some students refuse to cooperate with each other.	Don't panic. Encourage people to sort things out if they can; allow pairs or groups to swap around and brief each other on what they have achieved so far.
Unproductive feedback sessions.	Be sensitive to class reaction and be content with one or two constructive points.
Cries of 'Boring!'.	Give the project a rest—do something completely different: bring in an outside visitor/speaker or organize a visit; invite suggestions for ways forward.

Figure 5

Multi-tasking

Developing the four skills

Your students may perform a wide variety of tasks during the different stages in a project which require the implementation of a wide range of skills and use of language. Skills and language are used and developed interdependently and cumulatively—not necessarily in any prescribed order. However, it is possible to anticipate to a certain extent the skills and language that may be required. It is also a good idea to keep a record of past projects so that the requirements of future projects may be more accurately predicted.

To this end the flowcharts on pages 26 and 27 provide a structure for the monitoring of skills, language, and activities which emerge from a project. No two projects will ever be the same and you will need to adapt the model to your class and the project. But there is a progression of skills which is characteristic of all project work and the benefit of this diagrammatic representation is that it illustrates the enormous potential of this approach to language learning. The first model (see Figure 6) provides examples of the elements that are likely to occur in each category. The blank flowchart (see Figure 7) is a photocopiable model which you can use to record or predict your own projects. The lists on pages 28 and 29 give further examples of the skills, language, and activities that you can expect to be generated in any given project. You may wish to add to these lists or create your own as you gain experience from the projects you have undertaken.

A project flowchart—multi-tasking and related skills

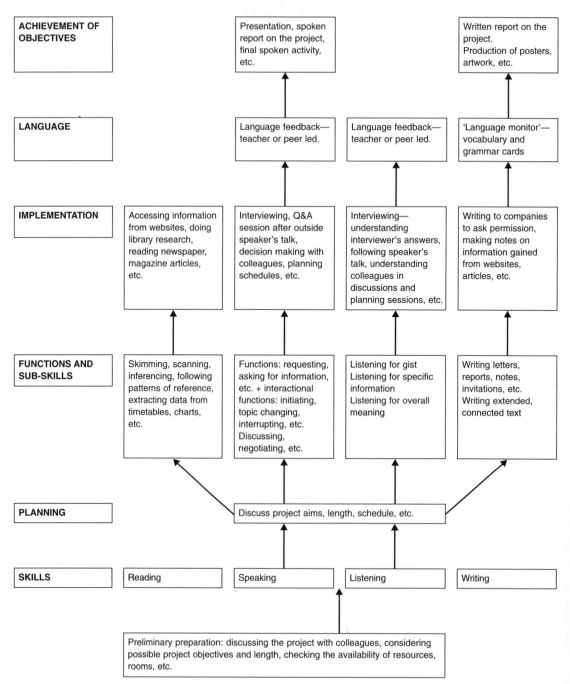

Figure 6

A project flowchart—multi-tasking and related skills

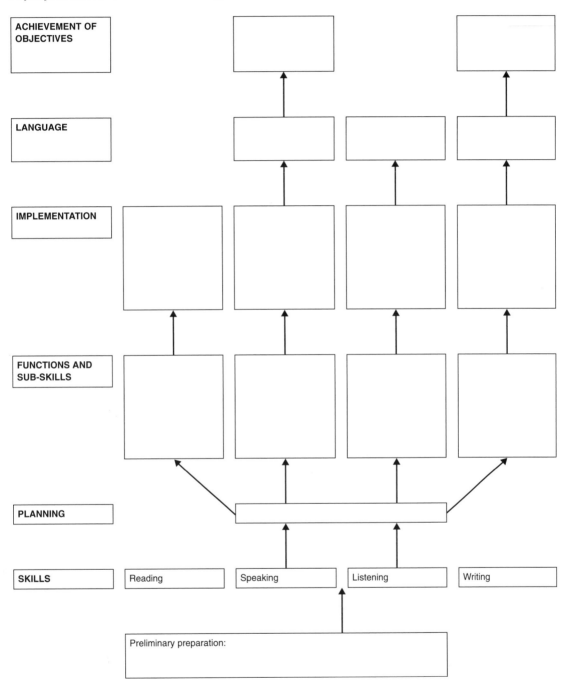

Figure 7

SPEAKING AND LISTENING

Project checklist

Functions	*Exponents*
Asking for information	Could you tell me ...?
Asking for opinions	What is your opinion on ...?
Agreeing/disagreeing	I'm not sure that I agree with you ...
Thanking	Many thanks.
Apologizing	I'm terribly sorry.

Interactional functions	*Exponents*
Initiating a conversation	Excuse me, do you have a couple of
(street interview)	minutes to spare?
Turn taking	If I could just say ...
Introducing and changing topic	But how about ...?
Dealing with difficult/hostile situations	Look, there's been a terrible misunderstanding ...

Sub-skills
Discussing
Negotiating
Presenting

Use of structures and vocabulary
Range of structures and vocabulary that can be used effectively and understood
Expanding this range through interaction with peers, teacher, project texts, encounters with
   native speakers
Consolidating this new language through the 'language monitor' and language feedback
   sessions

Project activities
Street interviews
Discussing project with group
Asking questions after a guest speaker's talk, understanding the answers
Talking to staff in shops, libraries, bus and train stations, etc.
Phone conversations with receptionists, information desk staff, etc.
Informal one-to-one interaction with team members

Practice activities
Language laboratory listening/drill practice
Role plays—short or extended
Watching authentic video for colloquial English listening practice
Visit to outside location with teacher before 'solo' visit

Support material
Cue cards for anticipated interactional situations
'Language monitor' cards
Information on transportation, safety advice, location of areas to be visited, etc.

WRITING AND READING

Project checklist

Functions Asking for information Inviting Asking for permission Making arrangements (for a visit, etc.)
Sub-skills Writing letters, emails, faxes, reports, scripts Note taking Summarizing Creating materials Reading for: gist global meaning specific information
Language Producing and recognizing written discourse—organizing of ideas, connecting ideas, linking stages of text, etc. Appropriate use of formality/informality Range of structures and vocabulary that can be used effectively and understood Expanding this range especially through exposure to texts encountered during the project Consolidating this new language through the 'language monitor' and language feedback sessions
Project activities Note taking from interviews, talks, written texts (websites, newspaper articles, magazines, etc.) Writing scripts for video production or radio recording Creating charts, diagrams, graphs, posters, etc. Designing questionnaires Using word processing and presentation software, e.g. Powerpoint Accessing information from websites Reading newspapers, journals, timetables, posters, advertisements, maps, letters, emails, faxes. Library research

Multi-tasking framework in action

The following project should be read in conjunction with the flowchart (Figure 8), checklists (page 32), and the Project Observation Record (Figure 9) as an illustration of how a project might be recorded.

Chinese bean sprouts

LEVEL	**Intermediate**
AGE RANGE	**Any age**
TIME	**4–6 days for the seeds to grow**
GENERAL AIMS	To record the growth of Chinese bean sprouts.
LANGUAGE AIMS	To use language to describe change, make comparisons, and report on progress; to communicate on the telephone.
LOCATION	Classroom; optional visit to a nursery or a garden centre.
RESOURCES	Seed catalogues or brochures, unless you want to buy the beans in advance; jam jars or glasses, muslin or cloth covers, and elastic bands; access to a water tap (the water has to be changed in the jars daily until the beans are ready to eat).

TEACHER PREPARATION

1 You will need either seed catalogues or a packet of seeds. One packet is sufficient for a whole class.

2 If you intend to visit a garden centre, this needs to be organized in writing and arrangements made beforehand. The excursion can take place before the introduction of the topic and serve as the stimulus for the project.

STUDENT PREPARATION

Students provide a jar or tumbler, an elastic band, and a piece of cloth to cover the top.

PROCEDURE

1 Introduce the topic using stimulus material such as pictures of Chinese food and seed catalogues. Play a guessing game based on the seed packet (conceal the name). Most packets carry background information, for example, that the Chinese have been growing bean sprouts for around 3,000 years and use them in a variety of savoury dishes and salads.

2 Encourage students to share their knowledge of any plants, herbs, fruit, or vegetables that may grow in their own gardens. Visit a garden centre, if you intend to do so.

3 Students work in pairs or small groups to observe the growth of the beans, to check their daily progress, and to report in writing about them (see Project Observation Record).

4 Students can display their written findings on a wall display.

FOLLOW-UP   This will depend on what has come out of students' work and whether it is appropriate to extend the language work further. For example, you could encourage students to find recipes which include bean sprouts and extend the language of instruction.

VARIATION   This project can be carried out with anything that can be grown indoors in compost, soil, or water.

COMMENTS   This is a very simple project which nevertheless generates a wide range of language skills.

The 'Chinese bean sprouts' project flowchart

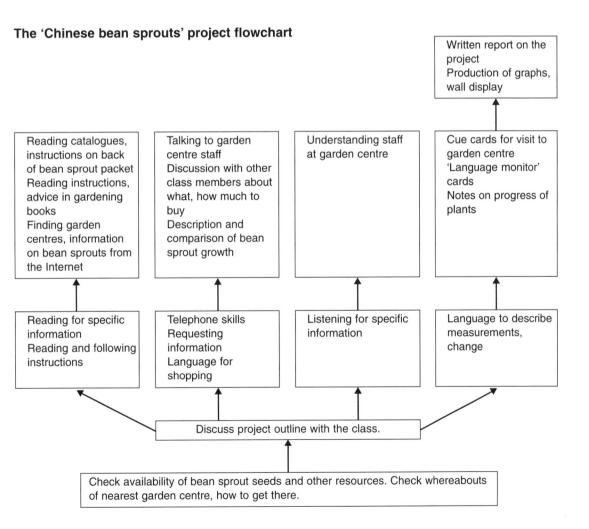

Figure 8

SPEAKING AND LISTENING

'Chinese bean sprout' project checklist

Functions	*Exponent*
Opening a telephone conversation	Hello. I'm calling about ...
Asking for information	Could you tell me ...?
	Do you have any other ...?
Initiating a conversation	Excuse me, could you help me ...?
Introducing a topic	I'm looking for ...
Terminating a conversation (phone and face-to-face)	Thanks for your help. (Bye.)
Understanding instructions	First, make a line of small ...

Sub-skills
Making telephone calls

Use and understanding of structures and vocabulary	
Describing change	These have grown two centimetres ...
Making comparisons	Team A's bean sprouts are the tallest.
Understanding native speakers	

Project activities
Talking to garden centre staff
Making phone calls
Discussion with other class members about what, how much to buy

Support material
Cue cards for visit to the garden centre

WRITING AND READING

Functions
Cue cards for visit to garden centre

Sub-skills
Reading catalogues, seed packet instructions, gardening books
Skimming, scanning, finding information
Accessing information from websites
Designing graphs and wall displays

Use and understanding of structures and vocabulary	
Describing change	These have grown two centimetres ...
Making comparisons	Team A's bean sprouts are the tallest.
Progress reports	We have finished planting ...

PROJECT OBSERVATION RECORD

Name .... **Date** .... **Class** ....

Name of plant ....

Date planted ....

Special instructions ....

Special observations ....

Graph showing growth rate

Height

Dates

Drawings

1 week	2 weeks	3 weeks	Fully grown

Figure 9

A final word

This new edition has been made possible thanks to all the teachers who took the time and trouble to send in their projects. Reading through the sheer number and variety of the projects has been both fascinating and exciting: fascinating because of the ways project work is transformed by individual teachers and their students, exciting because what is happening is so creative and innovative.

Every project in this book has been tried and tested. I am enormously grateful to all the teachers who have been willing to share their ideas and their expertise.

1 Media

1.1 School magazine

This project involves students in finding out what issues are of concern to local people by interviewing them and then writing about them in their own school magazine.

LEVEL	**Elementary and above**
AGE RANGE	**14–16 years**
TIME	**Flexible** (depending on how much time you want to devote to the project and the size of the end-product)
GENERAL AIMS	To produce a school magazine based on local issues.
LANGUAGE AIMS	To develop all four language skills by using interviewing techniques, telephone calls, and writing letters and articles; to learn vocabulary specific to the topics covered.
LOCATION	Students will need to interview local people.
RESOURCES	A variety of local newspapers and magazines; maps of the locality; camera; paper; dictionaries for class use; computer (optional), printer, and photocopying facilities.
TEACHER PREPARATION	1 Collect a variety of newspapers and magazines for your students.
	2 Obtain permission from the parents and the school for your students to interview people outside the class. Make sure they are covered by insurance.
STUDENT PREPARATION	As the magazine will be based on local issues, students will need to listen to or watch local/regional news programmes regularly and find out what is of topical interest to people in the area by reading local newspapers.
PROCEDURE	1 Introduce the topic and put students in small groups of about four or five.
	2 Students need to look at different newspapers and magazines as a stimulus for their own ideas. Some students may be more interested in one section than another. Allow them to browse and decide which aspects interest them.

3 They decide which group will take responsibility for the different sections of the magazine and which individuals will be responsible for carrying out interviews, writing articles, taking photographs, drawing pictures, designing the cover, etc.

4 Ask students to brainstorm a name for their magazine. Once they have decided on the various responsibilities and chosen a name, they will need to gather information relevant to their locality. This can be done independently, out of class time, or as part of their lesson time depending on your circumstances.

5 In order to gather information, students will have to make contact with people they wish to interview. This will involve letter-writing or making phone calls. At this stage it is unlikely that students will be using English, so help them to translate information they need to share with the rest of the class.

6 Students spend time interviewing, reading, writing, illustrating, taking photographs, etc., in/out of class time. Agree a deadline with the groups for completion of the contributions.

7 When all the material has come in, students collate the information and organize their contributions. It may be necessary for one or two students to exercise editorial control and decide on the order of features and how each page will look. If your students have access to computers and the necessary IT skills, they can set the texts and arrange the page layout electronically.

8 It is not necessary to rely on computers as writing/typing articles, including all the appropriate artwork, can be done manually and is likely to involve more students in the hands-on process. The finished product may not look quite as sophisticated but providing the text is produced clearly, using black ink, it will photocopy satisfactorily and can be stapled together so that each student has his/her own copy of the final magazine.

9 Offer copies to other classes to read. This will give students a greater sense of satisfaction in their achievement.

FOLLOW-UP

As the magazine begins to take shape, encourage your students to exchange ideas in English as far as possible. Ensure that what is being written is as accurate as possible. This will require your monitoring and intervention at various points. However, it will be less intrusive if you monitor students' spoken English and keep a discreet record of points to be worked on at a later date by the whole class if you realize that a particular set of errors is being made by a number of students.

VARIATION

Younger students could adopt the same approach but aim to produce a newsletter. Interviewees would need to be invited to the school for their interviews and students would be more restricted in exploring the locality and taking photographs.

COMMENTS	This kind of project is best carried out within a concentrated time frame, say, one week, or spread over two or three weeks. The longer the time span, the less topical some of the features will be.

Acknowledgements
Many thanks to Andrea Cecilia Coviella, Buenos Aires, Argentina for the original idea.

1.2 Making a radio programme

In this project students record their own radio programme based on recent current affairs and news topics.

LEVEL	Advanced
AGE RANGE	Adult
TIME	1 week
GENERAL AIMS	To record a five-minute current affairs/news programme for the radio.
LANGUAGE AIMS	To practise reading and writing skills; to have extended speaking practice (using a script).
LOCATION	Libraries, newsagents, students' homes.
RESOURCES	Tape recorders; cue cards; a computer with access to the Internet.
TEACHER PREPARATION	Record a current affairs/news programme which can act as a model for students' own programme.
STUDENT PREPARATION	Students need to collect newspapers and magazines, to watch television or listen to radio programmes, and to access news sites on the Internet.
PROCEDURE	1 Students work in small groups and coordinate their website searches and purchases of newspapers and magazines. They need to decide on each member's role: an overall presenter (anchorman/woman), and the different presenters for sport, weather, travel, etc.
	2 Using the materials the group has collected, students next write a tapescript for the programme. Each presenter takes responsibility for writing his/her own insert in the programme. The checking and revision can be shared.

Students will need to time their inserts very carefully so that the bulletin is the required length. As the work progresses, they will get an idea of how long it takes to read a certain number of words, so the time available for each contribution can be calculated and the writing edited if necessary.

3 When students are satisfied with the tapescript, they record their programme. The presenter introduces and links the items, using cue cards to cue in each reader.

4 When all the groups have finished recording, students then listen to each other's programmes. While they listen, students should make notes on what they thought was particularly interesting or anything they couldn't understand. You should also monitor students' performance.

5 After all the groups' programmes have been 'broadcast', as a class or in mixed groups, students should give each other feedback.

FOLLOW-UP

The programmes can be re-recorded if the students wish to improve on their performances. Depending on the results of your monitoring, you may wish to do remedial work on any areas of the students' use of language that you thought were weak.

VARIATION

If you have access to a video camera, for example, your students could produce a television news programme. In this case, the monitoring process would include body language and other aspects of visual presentation.

COMMENTS

This project can most easily be undertaken in an English-speaking environment where students can access up-to-date news and information. Alternatively, you can download information from the Internet, record a *BBC World Service* or *Voice of America* broadcast, video *CNN* or *BBC World* news bulletins if these are available. In order for the content to remain topical, the project is short and fairly intensive.

Acknowledgements
Many thanks to Pat McLoughlin, Internexus, Regent's College, London, England for the original idea.

1.3 My newspaper

This project extends and supports students' creative writing skills by giving them the opportunity to write their own newspaper articles and stories.

LEVEL

Intermediate

AGE RANGE

Older adolescent

TIME	Approximately 4 weeks (6–10 hours)

GENERAL AIMS — To produce a student newspaper based on the model of an English-language newspaper.

LANGUAGE AIMS — To develop intensive and extensive reading skills; to write newspaper articles based on the sample material.

LOCATION — Any library which stocks English-language newspapers. Some of the written work will be done at home.

RESOURCES — Samples of different broadsheet and tabloid newspapers written in English, such as the *Indian Express*, the *Hindu*, the *Bangkok Post*, the *China Daily*, the *Straits Times*, the *Washington Post*, *South China Morning Post*, *Sydney Morning Herald*, *The Times*, *Mirror*, the *Independent*, the *Guardian*, or the *Guardian Weekly* (the newspapers do not have to be UK publications); sample newspaper materials downloaded from the Internet; copies of enough material for your class to see how headlines are used, how different articles are structured, and where advertisements feature.

TEACHER PREPARATION — You need to buy or collect English-language newspapers.

STUDENT PREPARATION — Ask your students to bring in copies of newspapers in their own language.

PROCEDURE

1 If you had difficulty getting enough material together for the whole class, spread the sample material around the room and get students to look at it by walking around. They begin by studying several different kinds of newspapers, looking at their layout, their political views, how much space they devote to coverage of local, national, and international news, sport, culture, television reviews, etc.

2 Students need to scan the newspaper headlines in order to select an article which sounds interesting. They may find headlines difficult to understand. Before they can devise their own they may need you to point out that headlines rely on key words. They then skim the text to get the gist and if necessary use a dictionary to read the article in detail.

3 Once they have familiarized themselves with the way newspapers are structured, students work alone or in small groups to compare and discuss how the content of the different newspapers is organized.

4 Tell students to choose some of the articles as models for their own versions and to write their articles at home (see the examples of students' articles on pages 40–41). Set a deadline for completion of the articles.

UNITED KINGDOM *MIRROR* 40 p

AIDS OUT OF CONTROL

AIDS problem caued deadt of lots of

people over the world. About 11 man, women and children are infected every minute and last year 2.5 million people died. Infection is rising everywhere, also in the countries which could afford drugs to keep the diseas under control. And what is the most said information about this illness is that half of the 5.8 million people infected by the HIV virus last year were children and young people. They were infected through sex, dirty illness or were born to women with HIV. This infection is rising . Every man should think about this problem and tries to solve this problem by not taking any risk and behave responsibly.

" Radical therapy "

GOVERNMENT'S NEW "HELPFUL" PLAN

This new government plan changes the life of our disabled neighbours. The government wants to cut 175 million from spending on disability benefits. It will make the life of disabled people more difficult than it is now.

TURKEY'S WAR

Kurdish querrila leader Abdulah Ocalan highlighted Turkey's brutal war to suppress Kurdish rights. Turkish army and police lead war against Kurdish people. European Commission report said about torture in police stations, disappearances, and extra-judicial executions. The army also destroyed villiges and caused evacuations. It is quite difficult to understand why Turkish are not able to recognise this minority, if they could recognise Greeks, Jews, and Armenians. Are they less people than the others??? How it is possible that they cannot have their own schools, TV or radio stations, if other minorities can? And what about the world, why the countries do not try to help Kurds, but try to solve the problems in Kosovo, which is not worse than this suppress of one nation.

SPORT in brief

Olympic Games
Rod McGeoch, the director of the organising committee for Sydney 2000 Games, had to resigne. He said he was the victim of rumour-mongering. His leaving caused internal detabilisation and political and personal animoity.

Criket
Pakistan beat Zimbabwe by 111 runs in the third day of match. Pakistan's Ijaz Ahmed Won the Man of the Match award for his innings of 132 and Saeed Anwar contributed 73

GOOD MORNING *Thursday, January, 1998, 10SK*

National News
New Government won after
long fight against guerrilas,
whose leader Thomas Moon,
was arrested 2 days ago. Now
Legoland is free country.

WHO IS ROBIN HOOD

This is the question for all of us. Who is the man who robbed the National bank and gave money to all homeless people. There were 2 millions of corunas. During this crime nobody was killed or hurt. The Police asks for help and the bank offers award of 100, 000 corunas to anyone who can decribe this man and help to identify him. But as we know, no one gives any information about him. His behaving remembers us famous British holdup man Robin Hood, who fought against rich.

by Mike Nash

Rasto Najdev is the man who stole Mona Lias

Young man from East was yesterday arrested on suspicion of stoling
Mona Lias, one of the most famous paintings of the world. Thi picture
used to hung in the Legoland´s National Museum for centuries.
The police does not know where the picture is, but they hope that the young
tells them where is it and they also want to know the names of his companions.

GERGE MATHILSEN
NEW TENNIS CHAMPION

Young talented tennis player
Gerge Mathilsen became the
Younget tennis champion in
Paris, where he beat Ion Morris,
number 1 in ATP. This young
man, or better boy, is only 14
and is copmpared with other famous tennis player Matt Wilson.

10 PEOPLE KILLED BY AVALANCHE

Yesterday 10 people were killed in Austria by avalanche. Rescuers saved 20 people, but 10 people have been under snow. The chief recuer told us that there is no chance that they could survive.

5 The newspaper can be compiled individually or collaboratively. If it is to be a joint effort, students can take responsibility for contributing different articles, based on what has interested them in the original newspapers. Try to ensure a good coverage of topics.

6 Set a time for bringing all the materials together. Students then compile the newspaper.

7 Depending on the resources available, the newspapers can be reproduced for students from other classes to read, or they can be displayed on the classroom walls.

FOLLOW-UP

Students are likely to encounter a lot of new vocabulary in the course of their reading, some of which they may be able to incorporate into their articles.

VARIATION 1

The project can be adapted for use with different levels. At elementary level, students can prepare short articles with illustrations cut out from real newspapers. They can also draw their own cartoons and supply the captions and speech bubbles.

VARIATION 2

If you are working in an English-speaking environment, students can prepare a questionnaire which they use to interview local people about anything newsworthy. These interviews then constitute the basis for written articles incorporating direct speech.

COMMENTS

1 This kind of project encourages students to work independently. Initially, however, they may need a lot of support in getting to grips with the foreign newspapers. You have to decide how much material to put in front of them so that they are not overwhelmed by the volume of unfamiliar reading material.

2 Some students are better than others at looking up new vocabulary and are not afraid of making mistakes in their written work. Discuss these problems with your students and let them know you are aware of their difficulties. As with all projects, a real sense of achievement comes with displaying and sharing the end-product.

Acknowledgements
Many thanks to Eva Stradiotova, Bratislava, Slovakia for the original idea.

1.4 Audio guide

In this project students produce an audiotape with an accompanying illustrated handout for tourists to use on a sightseeing tour of a city.

LEVEL

Intermediate and above

AGE RANGE

Adolescent

TIME

8–10 lessons over 6–8 weeks

GENERAL AIMS

To produce an audiotape to accompany a walking tour of a city; to provide illustrated text to accompany the audiotape (optional).

LANGUAGE AIMS

To develop and extend speaking and writing skills.

LOCATION

Classroom for writing and recording; visits to the places students want to include in their recording and to libraries, museums, etc.

RESOURCES

Map of the city; camera(s); magazines/brochures to cut up; word-processing facilities; tape recorder and microphone; CD or taped music for sound effects.

TEACHER PREPARATION

1 At the start of the project check that your school/college is willing for students to go out to look at places of interest. Also ensure you have parental permission and insurance cover.

2 If this is impossible, agree the topic of the project with the students and ask them to organize themselves to research places in their own time and bring their suggestions to the first lesson.

3 Find out whether the local tourist office is interested in making use of the final recording.

STUDENT PREPARATION

Students check out places of interest and have information and a list of suggestions ready for the first lesson.

PROCEDURE

1 In the first session pool all the ideas and suggest students work in small groups on places of their choice. Encourage discussion in English.

2 Decide with your students whether the project will have a single focus and concentrate on an audiotape, or whether they want to produce accompanying illustrated text. If they choose the latter option, they need to agree who does what in each group. The illustrated text is likely to mirror the audio recording, so students must liaise carefully with each other.

3 Students decide on the sequencing of tour stops. Each group takes responsibility for a different place, so number the groups according to the tour sequence. A more advanced class can consider the links between places and write their script accordingly.

4 Each group drafts their section of the tapescript. Depending on the level and time available, students can concentrate on factual detail or add other information to their script.

Make sure you give each group a word count limit so that they all work within a prescribed time frame when it comes to the recording.

5 As students work on their tapescripts, monitor each draft and ask the students to check dates and factual information very carefully. Encourage peer-group correction as much as possible.

6 Rehearse the recordings. Practise pronunciation, stress, and rhythm, and make sure everyone speaks clearly and not too fast. Try to ensure that as many students are involved as possible.

Different students should contribute different sections. You may also want to include a presenter who introduces the recording, links the items, and concludes it.

7 Record the audiotape in a quiet environment. The recording can be done in stages, so try to avoid times when lesson bells ring. You may have to re-record if there are unexpected interruptions, sneezes, or coughs! Add sound effects and music if the students wish.

8 If students have chosen to produce illustrated text, ask them to finalize it.

9 Arrange for other classes to hear the audiotape if they wish and also offer it to the local tourist office.

FOLLOW-UP

The written tapescript and the spoken recording are likely to provide further opportunities for developing accuracy and fluency.

VARIATION 1

Students can role-play historical events involving the city, write and dramatize a short sketch, interview a historical figure, etc.

VARIATION 2

The project lends itself to making a video recording if you have the equipment—with a voice-over if you are really ambitious!

Acknowledgements
Many thanks to Ewa Przezdziecka at Primary School No. 319, Warsaw, Poland, and Marcia Antonia Cia Ribeiro Santos, Collegio Rio Branco, Campinas, Brazil for the original idea.

1.5 A brochure for new students

In this project students produce a guide to the local area for other students in their school.

LEVEL	**Elementary to lower-intermediate**
AGE RANGE	**Any age**
TIME	**3 hours a week over 12 weeks**

GENERAL AIMS To produce a short brochure with up-to-date information about local shops, transportation, museums, and restaurants.

LANGUAGE AIMS To learn the survival language skills necessary for coping with daily life when settling into a new environment; to use survival phrases, such as *I'm sorry, could you repeat that, please?*, to practise and use common questions using *How much ...? How far ...?*, etc.

LOCATION Local tourist office, bus and railway stations, museums, food markets, places of interest in the locality.

RESOURCES Information leaflets, transport timetables, etc.; clipboards or notebooks; a minibus if available; coloured folders; word-processing facilities if available.

TEACHER PREPARATION Make sure students can find their way in and around the area, have enough money for bus fares, have sufficient grasp of survival phrases and common questions, such as *How much is a single to the town centre?*, and are willing to accept the idea of studying outside the classroom. Having established these, students should be encouraged to work as independently as possible.

STUDENT PREPARATION Students familiarize themselves with the local area during their free time.

PROCEDURE An average week might go like this:

1 Arrange transport and a time convenient for students to leave the classroom.

2 Students learn essential vocabulary and phrases and rehearse these through role-play if necessary.

3 Accompany or deliver students to the bus/train station, museum, market, etc., and arrange to meet them at a specific time and place. Make sure they always work in pairs or small groups.

4 Encourage students to buy their own tickets and to function independently by reading information screens, notices, etc., and asking appropriate people, such as bus drivers or museum staff, for help rather than relying on you. Collect leaflets, timetables, advertisements, etc.

5 Return to school/college and store material in folders kept in the classroom or on the premises so that nothing gets lost. The material needs to be sorted out before being stored in folders and each folder needs to be labelled depending on the material that has been collected. Different coloured folders would be helpful. Sample folders might include: *Places to visit, Food and drink, Entertainment, Transport and timetables.*

6 Students select appropriate information and copy this onto the page which will go into the final brochure. They can include additional information which they have gained from personal experience. For example, certain trains may be very crowded at particular times, a bus journey may take longer during the rush hour, and some shops may stay open late on certain days.

FOLLOW-UP

Editing and checking information to include in the final brochure; updating information if appropriate. At a later stage, interviews could be set up with people who work in various establishments and these can form the basis of another project.

VARIATION 1

Using the same procedure, students with access to a camera can take photographs which could either be scanned into a brochure or displayed as a wall presentation in the classroom.

VARIATION 2

This approach could be adapted for a group of foreign students who are visiting your town or city. The information would then need translating into English before it could be produced in brochure form.

COMMENTS

1 In some cases, students may have more computer skills than their teachers. In these circumstances teachers can exploit a genuine communication gap if they are intending to produce a word-processed brochure. Many students find this activity very motivating, particularly when they see an end-product they have helped to create. Some of the handwritten material may be scrapped if the information is being stored on disk. The production process is less time-consuming if information is transferred directly onto a computer in the first place. If students have access to computers outside classroom teaching time, they are often motivated to work on their own or help other students who may be less confident working on a computer.

2 Overall this activity is an excellent way to encourage elementary learners to develop their confidence and language skills. It brings variety into the classroom and students appreciate the opportunities to make an equal contribution to their own learning programme.

Acknowledgements
Many thanks to Raymond Hoey and Jenny Reynolds at Bradford College English Language Centre, Yorkshire, England for the original idea.

1.6 Staff portrait gallery

In this project students interview and take photos of the staff at their school, write short profiles, and display the results in their classroom.

LEVEL	**Intermediate**
AGE RANGE	**13–18 years**
TIME	**Approximately 8 hours plus students' own time**

GENERAL AIMS To produce a display featuring photos and profiles of the school staff.

LANGUAGE AIMS To use question forms and reported speech; to practise listening and writing skills.

LOCATION The school premises.

RESOURCES A camera or cameras, ideally Polaroid (optional—students can draw or sketch staff portraits); large sheets or stiff paper or card; glue (or pins) to display photos and text.

TEACHER PREPARATION

1 Before the project, establish that the staff do not mind being photographed or interviewed.

2 Find examples of profiles of people (celebrities, etc.) from newspapers and magazines which include photos and personal details.

STUDENT PREPARATION None.

PROCEDURE

1 Show students some examples of people's profiles from newspapers or magazines and highlight the sort of information that is included.

2 Either as a whole class exercise or working in small groups, brainstorm the names and positions of staff, including secretaries, cleaners, caretakers, etc.

3 Ask students to decide who they would like to do profiles on, making sure that they include a variety of people from around the school. They then make a list of questions they would like to ask—these may be general or individualized for particular members of staff. These questions can then be pooled and discussed, and practised in role-plays.

Encourage students to limit their questions to three or four per person and to write open-ended questions, i.e. questions which cannot be answered with just *yes* or *no*. Elicit some examples:

– How long have you been teaching at this school?
– What do you like to do in the holidays?
– What is your favourite television programme?

4 Draw up a schedule with the groups for interviews and photographs and agree a deadline. Don't allow too long or the project will lose impetus.

5 Each group then interviews and photographs as per the schedule and assembles their material. Notes should be taken during the interview or answers written down verbatim. (See Figure 10.)

Figure 10   Staff portrait gallery

6 After the interviews the answers should be adapted into profiles. These should be self-edited where possible but check the final results. An example:

This is Kurt Wiedermannn. He teaches chemistry and has been here for six years. He is married with two children and plays the guitar in his spare time.

Encourage peer-group correction by having each group exchange their short texts. The final 'gallery' can be assembled when each group has finished and put them up on the wall for everyone to see and read.

FOLLOW-UP   Monitor students for their use of question forms and reported speech, and give further practice if these structures caused any breakdown in communication.

VARIATION 1   The project could also be done as a students' gallery.

VARIATION 2   It could also be displayed in a public area of the school.

COMMENTS   This is a good way for people to get to know each other at the beginning of a new term or year.

This project was devised by the author.

2 Culture

2.1 Protecting the environment

This project draws on young students' experiences of their local environment and centres on producing a magazine focusing on environmental issues.

LEVEL	**Elementary**
AGE RANGE	**Young adolescent**
TIME	**6 × 2-hour lessons**
GENERAL AIMS	To produce a magazine dealing with ways of protecting the environment and suggesting possible solutions to the problems of pollution, destruction of the rainforests, and the environment in general.
LANGUAGE AIMS	To extend students' vocabulary through topic-specific reading; to write short articles on the environment; to devise or translate headlines for the magazine.
LOCATION	Classroom and library.
RESOURCES	Recycled paper for the magazine; pictures and photographs cut out of magazines or photocopied if absolutely essential; articles on environmental issues can be downloaded from the Internet if necessary.
TEACHER PREPARATION	1 Decide with the class which topics are of interest to them and either supply the reading material yourself or ensure that students can be relied on to bring the materials to the lessons.
	2 Ask students to read the information at home and to bring summaries of their articles together with pictures and photographs to the lesson. Unless your students already know how to write a summary, work through a sample exercise with them in class and provide a clear framework for them to follow. If this work is done in their mother tongue, allow time for key information to be translated.
STUDENT PREPARATION	At this level, students are most likely to read the articles they want to use in their mother tongue. In this case, it is best if you ask students to summarize an article and then consider translating the summaries at a later date. Ask students to work

in small groups when it comes to translation and refine the translations yourself if you feel it is necessary.

PROCEDURE

1 Divide students into small groups according to their interests, for example, pollution in cities, animals in danger, etc., and tell them to read the appropriate articles which you and they have collected.

2 Within their groups students choose the most interesting summaries to include in the final magazine. Allow each group the same amount of space, so that they have to combine text and pictures to fit and to represent their particular interest.

3 When the planning stage is complete each group writes up their contribution. In discussion with the class, choose one or two individuals to number the pages, finalize the sequence of the materials, and write the contents page and the list of contributors.

4 Display the magazine in a central area, such as the school foyer, so that other students can read it. If your school has a website, this is one way of reaching a wider audience.

FOLLOW-UP

At this level your students will probably have used their mother tongue while working together on the magazine. You could use this stage of the project to present some elementary language strategies for working together, perhaps with a view to putting such strategies into practice on another project.

VARIATION

The topic of the environment is vast and is applicable to all levels. An advanced class could choose just one aspect, such as the threat to the rainforests, and produce a magazine dealing with the subject in depth.

COMMENTS

1 Students involved in this project took part in a national magazine-writing campaign. Altogether 3,500 magazines were produced by different groups of students throughout the country.

2 Some of the language skills emerging from this project will be determined by the translation work which needs to be done. Depending on the level and ability of your class, you may not want them to do more than devise headlines for the different texts and write captions for the photographs in English. Nevertheless, there is likely to be a good deal of new vocabulary which your students are going to want to record (see 'Language Monitor' on page 16).

Acknowledgements
Many thanks to Rosana Beatriz Zublin, The Milky Way Institute of English, Rio Negro, Argentina for the original idea.

2.2 Clean up your area

**In this project students look at environmental issues in
their own homes and produce a local newsletter and an
art exhibition on these issues.**

LEVEL	**Elementary**
AGE RANGE	**Older adolescent and above**
TIME	**1–2 hours a week over 4–6 weeks**

GENERAL AIMS

To raise awareness of local environmental issues; to produce a
newsletter for distribution and an exhibition (optional) for
display within the school.

LANGUAGE AIMS

To develop students' overall language skills and to learn new
vocabulary; to devise questionnaires, write formal letters, carry
out interviews, practise asking questions, collate information,
take notes, translate and edit material, and write text appropriate
for a newsletter.

LOCATION

School and library for research purposes.

RESOURCES

Access to the Internet (if possible); photocopying facilities;
camera(s); display boards; large sheets of card/paper, coloured
pens, glue, scissors, etc.

**TEACHER
PREPARATION**

1 Ensure that students are familiar with the topic-specific
vocabulary of environmental issues. They may already know
this vocabulary or you may need to introduce it through
stimulus material and/or discussion.

2 You also need to establish whether there are local 'green'
organizations in your area, such as *Ecological Club, Our Earth,
Greenpeace, Earthwatch, Friends of the Earth*, etc., for stage 3 of
the project.

3 See if it is possible to get an English-speaking environmental
expert to come and talk to your students.

**STUDENT
PREPARATION**

Students prepare questions to ask their families on recycling
habits. During the project, they also read background
information, and collect pamphlets, brochures, photos, and
pictures for their exhibition.

PROCEDURE

1 Introduce the topic and tell students they are going to
devise a questionnaire to use individually as a means of
monitoring what happens to waste materials in their own
homes and how much use is made of recycling bins. If
families do not use different bins for recycling clear glass,

coloured glass, paper, tins, etc., students can be asked to monitor the amount and type of waste that accumulates each week. Help students with the questionnaire if necessary.

2 Students bring in the information and work on this 'Family Fact File' questionnaire in small groups. The class pool their ideas and produce a poster with a large-scale questionnaire, diagrams, charts, tables, pictures, photographs, and sample materials, etc. This can be displayed in the classroom, showing the information collected from the whole class during the course of one week.

3 Before students start writing their newsletter, give them the names of environmental organizations to contact. Some of these may provide publicity information, visiting speakers, video materials, posters for display, etc. Based on this information, students will later write articles for a newsletter or magazine about environmental issues affecting the area where they live.

Try to contact a speaker who is willing to talk to your students in English. Alternatively, you or your students may know of local journalists who speak English and who are interested in environmental issues. One or more of them might be willing to talk to the students.

Prior to engaging visiting speakers, students need to get more detailed background information as a basis for classroom discussion. In this way, students are in a better position to prepare informed questions to put to a speaker. Background information is best collected by students working in small groups. They can decide which group visits a library, uses the Internet, interviews an expert, etc.

4 If the students have collected information in a language other than English, some of the material may have to be translated. Help your students to decide what is relevant and likely to make an interesting newsletter.

5 Once students have all the information, they start writing their newsletter. Each group takes responsibility for a different section. Suggest that each group appoints someone to be in charge of layout, illustrations, typing up, etc.

6 (Optional) If your students have collected a vast amount of information and material, much of which cannot be included in the newsletter, they might be able to set up an exhibition if space is available.

FOLLOW-UP

The suggested variations (see below) provide opportunities for students to work on descriptive language in order to explain the art exhibits. 'Variation 2' gives students the opportunity to learn the kind of language used for writing and answering formal invitations for an authentic occasion.

VARIATION 1

Rubbish as Art If your students are interested in art, they could organize an exhibition to show how things typically thrown away can be turned into art.

VARIATION 2

Green disco If your students are really enthusiastic, they could organize a themed disco. Using green paper, they write invitations to their friends, parents, and other people who have played a role in the project. Everyone has to wear green clothes and students prepare green food and drink. Obviously, their work can be on display and they can play music by artists who are sympathetic to green issues.

COMMENTS

The starting point for this particular project was the Australian *Clean Up The World* campaign. The whole school might be interested in participating in a poster competition to promote the *Clean Up The World* campaign. However, any environmental topic which is relevant to your students could act as the starting point for a project.

Acknowledgements
Many thanks to Ewa Przezdziecka, Primary School No. 319, Warsaw, Poland for the original idea.

2.3 Drugs: Only mugs do drugs

This project aims to increase students' awareness of the problems associated with drugs.

LEVEL

Upper-intermediate and above

AGE RANGE

Older adolescent and above

TIME

Approximately 12 hours over 4 weeks (flexible)

GENERAL AIMS

To increase awareness of issues surrounding drugs and drug abuse, from cigarettes to hard drugs, through a variety of media.

LANGUAGE AIMS

To extend students' vocabulary related to drugs and contemporary slang; to give extensive reading practice in different genres and extensive fluency practice including discussion/presentation giving.

LOCATION

Library, a video shop.

RESOURCES

Trainspotting* by Irvine Walsh (novel and film); *Junkie* by William S Burroughs (novel); *Junk* by Melvyn Burgess (novel); the Internet; *Time Magazine* (US) June 5, 2000 Vol. 155 No. 23; dictionaries.

TEACHER PREPARATION

1 Collect some of the material itemized under 'Resources', or your own authentic source material. Whatever you decide, this project initially relies on being able to present your students with stimulating material.

2 If possible, arrange for an outside speaker, for example a member of staff from a drop-in centre.

STUDENT PREPARATION

1 Ask your students to bring in any article or information they have on drugs. These materials which they will have researched in a library will most probably be in their mother tongue. It is a good idea to alert students to this topic well in advance, so that time can be allowed for them to collect magazine and newspaper cuttings, advertisements, watch related television programmes, listen to the radio for similar relevant programmes, etc.

2 If you arrange for an outside speaker, students need to prepare questions in advance. Divide the class into small groups, so that each group focuses on one discussion point and is then responsible for translating that aspect of the discussion into English for the rest of the class.

PROCEDURE

1 Students read and translate the materials they collect in small groups and share their translations with each other. These can be photocopied or alternatively pinned up for others to read. The same process can apply to researching information using the Internet (see page 120) and interviewing fellow students and teachers for their views on the subject.

2 Before all the data is collected, discuss with students the end-product they want to achieve—essays, posters, a panel discussion, or a presentation on the surveys carried out. (See Figure 11 for an example of student work.) There is no reason why small groups cannot work towards different end-products.

3 Monitor and assist students as they work on their project. Make sure that any work done is displayed on the wall or, in the case of presentations, that the other students participate as the audience, ask questions, and debate the topics raised. A chairperson should be appointed for the panel discussion.

FOLLOW-UP

Students can follow up the slang language they have learnt by working on more colloquial, idiomatic expressions and looking at which phrases can or can not be used in a given context.

VARIATION

This approach to a controversial topic could be used as a starting point for other related projects, such as street crime.

Figure 11

COMMENTS   Some students may know people who take drugs, in which case the situation must be handled very sensitively. You need to have the explicit cooperation of your students as well as parents and colleagues. It is not advisable to interact with people related to drugs outside the circle of people known to yourself or your students.

Trainspotting is a film dealing with drug addiction in Glasgow, Scotland. It contains violent scenes and abusive language and may be considered offensive by some people. If you have not seen the film, you should certainly watch it before showing it to your students. In the UK the film is restricted to adults aged 18 years and over. For similar reasons you should also check the language used in *Junkie* and *Junk*.

Acknowledgements
Many thanks to Marie Havlickova, Gymnazium Zlin, Lesni Ctvrt, Czech Republic for the original idea.

2.4 Cultural perspectives

This project focuses on students' own cultural identities, highlighting those aspects of their cultures that are important to them. It also enables them to introduce aspects of their culture to students of other nationalities and cultures.

LEVEL   **Elementary and above**

AGE RANGE   **Any age**

TIME   **6–8 lessons (but very flexible)**

GENERAL AIMS   To develop an end-product which can be used by students to inform others about their own or another culture; to foster a sense of independence and personal achievement.

LANGUAGE AIMS   To practise all four language skills; to practise the language of instruction using imperatives; to develop skimming and scanning reading strategies.

LOCATION   Libraries, museums, tourist offices, travel agents. How much your students need to work outside the classroom depends on the nature of their end-product.

RESOURCES   Large sheets of card, coloured pens, glue, scissors; access to computers, the Internet, CD-ROMs, encyclopaedias; camera(s), tape recorders; magazines to cut up.

TEACHER PREPARATION

1 The extent of your preparation depends on the kind of project you envisage. If students want to demonstrate their country's traditional food and cooking, it is likely to involve the purchase of some food ingredients. In this case, find out whether such a project is feasible from the practical and financial points of view before students become too enthusiastic about the idea. If students want to stage a performance of folk dancing, make sure you or they can supply the accompanying music!

2 The list of topic areas below has proved a useful source of ideas applicable to any country's culture.

- family life
- language
- music
- race
- religion
- the media
- employment

- education
- humour
- feasts and festivals
- curiosities
- politics
- sport and games
- tales and legends

STUDENT PREPARATION

Ask students to collect material before the start of a project or, if it involves contacting their own countries or other countries for information, you should allow time for this before the project.

PROCEDURE

1 Students work best in pairs or small groups on a topic area which interests them, so divide the class into groups and allow time for discussion and negotiation of topics.

2 Students research, assemble, and compile information from a range of sources, and translate relevant information if necessary.

Students intending to produce a poster with a strong visual theme will need to find pictures, photographs, illustrations, etc. The steps involved in a poster presentation include: looking at existing posters to decide what makes an effective poster; deciding on the content of the poster; collecting information and designing artwork; drafting text; correcting and rewriting text; deciding on picture and text layout; and mounting pictures and text.

3 Students working on a written assignment, such as a report, can follow whatever is appropriate in the following stages:

- choosing topic/title
- background reading and note taking
- preparing interviews/questionnaires
- conducting interviews
- transcribing notes or recordings
- writing up information in draft form
- checking and rewriting
- devising cover page, contents
- final presentation of project.

4 Encourage students working on more practical projects, such as cooking, dancing, teaching a folk song, etc. to record their ideas on paper. They should focus on giving instructions and directions so that they are able to give a clear oral account when it is their turn to present their project.

5 Monitor what each group is doing and provide support where necessary.

6 Draw up a programme for each group to present its project, varying the activities and allowing plenty of time so that everyone has a good opportunity to explain their work and answer questions about their various displays, etc.

FOLLOW-UP

1 Poster displays can be exploited by getting groups to read each other's posters, and following this up with a quiz to focus on relevant and interesting detail. Each group obviously writes its own quiz and checks other people's answers.

2 If local people have contributed to the project, students could prepare a summary of their project in the form of an information sheet which could be distributed to the different contributors. Invite the contributors to come and see the end-product.

3 An end-product might be worth advertising or displaying so that other students, teachers, and parents can see what has been achieved. Well-designed posters could be left up for a period of time. Any work on display is usually a source of pride and thus good for student morale.

4 Set up a cultural evening open to other students, parents, and colleagues and get students to design a programme which displays their own or other cultures' diversities. An evening which offers cooking and eating, with dance, music, and oral presentations is bound to be entertaining!

VARIATION

One or more groups could embark on a project which compares and contrasts two different cultures.

COMMENTS

This kind of project fosters students' sense of independence and achievement through setting their own goals and working towards a shared end-product. The experience usually enables students to discover their strengths in ways which might otherwise not emerge in the classroom.

Acknowledgements
Many thanks to Lucia-Juncal Manzno Molinedo, English Academy, Guadalajara, Spain; Marta Gabrysova, Basic School, Unicov, Czech Republic; Nikki Bennett-Williams, Monkton Combe School, Bath, England; and Desmond Burton, Elcos, University of Wales, Bangor, Wales for the original idea.

2.5 Holidays and festivals

In this project students present or demonstrate a feature of their own culture, or a culture they are interested in, related to customs and festivals.

LEVEL	Elementary to intermediate
AGE RANGE	13 years and above
TIME	8 × 40-minute lessons over approximately 8 weeks
GENERAL AIMS	To produce one or a combination of the following: a fact sheet; a poster; a performance, such as a song, a ceremony, or a dance; a short, illustrated talk.
LANGUAGE AIMS	To practise all four language skills.
LOCATION	Library (optional).
RESOURCES	Computers at home or at school with access to the Internet; a video camera or tape recorder (optional).
TEACHER PREPARATION	Make sure you are aware of the different nationalities of your students if you are teaching a multilingual group. Brief yourself on some of the festivals and customs that your students are likely to be familiar with. If you are teaching students of the same nationality, be aware that their mother tongue or religious background may differ.
STUDENT PREPARATION	Students collect introductory material on a festival or custom. They can interview family members, search websites at home or at school, bring in photographs, pictures, and anything related to the topic.
PROCEDURE	1 Students share their information with the rest of the class.

2 In pairs or small groups, students choose a particular custom or festival and collect more detailed information. Make sure students are aware of available resources even if they don't exploit all of them: reference books, encyclopedias, CD-ROMs, websites, etc.

3 Encourage students to talk to relatives or family friends who may have personal memories of various occasions. Records of these conversations will probably be in your students' mother tongue, so you may need to help with translations if some of the information is to form part of the end-product.

4 Students decide on their end-product. Check that what they choose to do is manageable within the time allocated to the project. Whatever end-product students choose, they write a

short introduction which they use to present their project to the rest of the class in order to explain its significance.

5 Draw up a programme which brings together all the contributions, making a note of the length of time each contribution will take. Don't try to fit too much into one lesson. Students will enjoy the occasion more if the atmosphere is relaxed and there is time for spontaneous feedback, questions, and comments.

Distribute copies of the programme with the title of each project and the names of the participants, and make sure everyone in the class has a copy.

FOLLOW-UP

Some of the presentations may be suitable for publishing on the Internet. Editing and revising work should involve other students who may also be able to add extra information.

VARIATION

This project could be condensed into a shorter time period, for example, on a short course, or extended to produce more detailed written work.

COMMENTS

In a mixed-ability ESL group, it is possible to pair students at different levels with each student concentrating on tasks that are appropriate to their language ability.

Acknowledgements
Many thanks to Maggie Hos-McGrane, International School of Amsterdam, the Netherlands for the original idea.

2.6 How green are you?

This project starts with students' immediate home environments and provides opportunities for them to engage in wider environmental issues.

LEVEL

Lower-intermediate to intermediate

AGE RANGE

Older adolescent

TIME

2 lessons a week over 2 weeks

GENERAL AIMS

To carry out a survey and report on the results.

LANGUAGE AIMS

To practise reported speech and comparative and superlative structures; to introduce students to topic-specific vocabulary and to give them practice in both oral and written English.

LOCATION

Classroom (can be extended outside the classroom).

RESOURCES Tape recorders (optional) for students to record their interviews and listen to their own pronunciation.

TEACHER PREPARATION

1 Prepare the questions students will use to interview each other (see page 64). It is essential that students understand the questions you have prepared for them.

2 Also ensure that they have mastered the rudiments of interviewing. Practise question forms and structures, such as *I'd like to ask you a few questions. Thank you very much.*

3 Unless your class is familiar with reported speech, pre-teach and practise direct and reported speech. Students also need to know comparative and superlative forms of adjectives and adverbs.

4 Introduce the topic in advance and encourage students each to bring one idea to contribute to the pre-project class discussion.

STUDENT PREPARATION Think of one idea to contribute to the discussion.

PROCEDURE

1 Explain the project and why students will be carrying out certain activities. Follow this up with a pre-project discussion on ecological issues.

2 Students interview each other, moving round the class and recording their interviewees' answers. They can record the responses directly on to the questionnaires by ticking *yes* or *no*. Encourage a monolingual class to use English as far as possible when they are doing their surveys and try to ensure this by monitoring students.

3 Ask a few students to report their findings orally to consolidate some of the language they have been using, and for you to check whether they are using reported speech structures correctly.

4 Students then summarize their results in the form of a graph or pie chart and expand this information with sentences such as:

   – *Five students said that they had used a bottle bank.*
   – *Seven students said they had never used a bottle bank.*
   – *More people use disposable pens than walk to school.*

5 The results of the survey can be displayed in a central area so that that everyone in the school can read them.

FOLLOW-UP The topic of ecology can be extended if students are interested and the same methodology can be applied to another survey.

VARIATION More advanced students can discuss a topic and write their own open-ended questions.

COMMENTS

In order to vary the pattern of results, ask students to interview students in another year group in the school. This can be done in a break or by liaising with colleagues beforehand, so that students are invited into another class.

Sample questionnaire
1 Do you buy canned drinks?
2 Do you sometimes drop litter in the street?
3 Do you use disposable pens?
4 Did you walk or cycle to school today?
5 Do you turn off unnecessary lights?
6 Do you think about noise pollution?
7 Do you write on both sides of a sheet of paper?
8 Have you read about the hole in the ozone layer?
9 Do you use plastic bags more than once?
10 Do you eat fast food?

Acknowledgements
Many thanks to Joanne Sintes, Holly House, British Language Centre, Madrid for the original idea.

2.7 'Mottainai' or in English, 'What a waste!'

This project uses information from an environmental organization based in Japan to encourage a variety of possible end-products.

LEVEL

Intermediate

AGE RANGE

Any age

TIME

15 minutes per class over 20 weeks (flexible)

GENERAL AIMS

To enable students to give an oral presentation and display their work to their parents; to increase environmental awareness. Students will become far more conscious of environmental issues within society as a result of exposure over a period of time to this kind of topic.

LANGUAGE AIMS

To practise and develop all four language skills.

LOCATION

Students visit anywhere which can provide additional information on their chosen topic.

RESOURCES

Television and video recorder; *Global Mottainai Movement* video; video camera; computer with access to the Internet.

TEACHER PREPARATION

1 Before the project, set up contacts and collect as much relevant material as possible. The Global Mottainai Movement is represented throughout the world, so it should be possible to arrange for a representative to talk to your students. You can also request newsletters and videos. Use these to introduce environmental issues (see Figure 12).

2 Depending on what your students know already, you may need to pre-teach topic-specific vocabulary.

3 Check whether it is feasible to send your students out of school in order to interview people in the street as well as families in their homes. Make sure students always go in pairs and that students are covered by insurance.

STUDENT PREPARATION

Collect material and do background reading. Students can access information via the Internet, look for articles in newspapers and magazines such as *Greenpeace*, watch television programmes, and listen to the radio.

PROCEDURE

1 If possible, show the class the *Global Mottainai Movement* video. If you invite a speaker from the Movement, organize a question-and-answer session, provided the speaker is notified in advance.

2 If they are going to interview people outside the classroom, students will need to rehearse and role-play interviewing techniques, even if they are going to conduct the interview in their mother tongue.

3 Divide the class into groups of four to six students. Throughout the following weeks, each group familiarizes itself with the topic through reading and discussion. Encourage them to share information with each other during the short slot that is devoted to the project in each lesson. They can look at each other's materials, brainstorm ideas, and discuss their findings. Eventually everyone has seen, read, or heard all the information, either directly or through shared group work. Warn them that they should shortlist items of interest which they would like to use as part of their final presentation in front of an audience.

4 Each group stockpiles material, ideas, pictures, and anything which may contribute to their end-product.

5 Each group decides on a format for their presentation: a chart, a poster, an illustrated talk using OHTs, a quiz, or a sketch. They then prepare and present it.

FOLLOW-UP

If you have a video camera, film the live presentations and use these recordings for follow-up work in class at a later stage. If students do not feel confident in front of a camera, recording their presentations should be optional. If appropriate, however, you could focus on one or two aspects of their performance,

Global Mottainai Movement

MOTTAINAI NEWS
No. 1

JUNIOR CHAMBER INTERNATIONAL

MOTTAINAI

Examples of practices of the Mottainai Movement throughout Japan

1. Bring to dinner tables vegetables not standardized or sorted but sold by the gram (Hokkaido District)

Standards are set for conveniences in distribution and sales, disregarding what should normally be required of "food"—freshness, safety and good taste. These standards lead to the production of vegetables that do not go to the market. In the Hokkaido area, we held display-and-sale fairs of u-sorted, fresh vegetables produced in Hokkaido in conformity with the objective of the Mottainai Movement, and conducted activities to promote that movement.

2. Eye bank and kidney bank registration promotion campaign (Morioka JC, Iwate Bloc, Tohoku District)

In Iwate Prefecture at present, cornea transplants could save about 200 patients, and kidney transplants about 1,000 patients. However, the annual registration campaign had not produced expected results. Therefore, Morioka JC conducted-a-campaign, as part of the Mottainai Movement to promote registrations with the eye bank and the kidney bank.

As a result, both banks received registration applications from more than 50 people during a period of a little over 2 months from the start of the campaign.

3. Use of rain water in Sumida-ward, Tokyo (Kanto District)

Sumida-ward depends on a dam about 150 kilometers upstream of the Tone River for its water resources. In recent years, however, the area has suffered damage from lack of water in summer, and in times of torrential rainfalls, had the problem of the urban flooding where rain water back-flowed because it could not seep into the ground. Therefore, Sumida-ward decided to take a different approach, and is now using the rain water falling in the area as a self-supplied water "resource."

To cite typical examples, the Sumida Ward Office and Ryogoku Kokugi-kan store the rain falling on the roofs of the buildings and use it for flush toilets and air-conditioning. Also, in the parks operated by the ward, there are water storage tanks to secure water supplies for fire fighting and drinking in case of an emergency.

4. Record Museum (Arita JC, Wakayama Bloc, Kinki District)

Wakayama Bloc, trying to create a "music record museum" to discover and preserve the culture of LP records which have completely disappeared as a result of the spread of the CD, started in June of 1993 to collect records.

About 1,000 records have already been collected

and these include some masterpieces produced in the 1960s and 1970s, the golden age of the LP, and rare disks not likely to be put on sale again. They plan to work to expand the collection to 50,000 disks.

5. Contest of compositions themed on intolerance to wasteful practices (Kyushu District)

The Kyushu District held a contest of compositions themed on intolerance to wasteful practices as part of the Mottainai campaign. The objective was to help encourage children, the main group of people to support our next generation, to think about their current lifestyle and have greater awareness as global citizens. The winners of the contest were announced and awarded at a ceremony held at the August 28-29 Kyushu District Convention.

6. Used coffee beans

A coffee shop at one particular hotel produces about 10 kg (enough for 500 cups) of used coffee beans each day. They used to throw them away as garbage, but now they scatter them in the service entrance and garbage storage area. This has the dual effect of controlling the odor of the garbage and keeping the cats away.

7. Food trays

Trays are used in enormous quantities for food items. There is much clamor against them as if they are the worst sources of environmental problems. However, trays are certainly very convenient. A company in Fukushima City, Hiroshima Prefecture is a major manufacturer of trays. The company collects the trays at the supermarkets and recycles them in practice of the Mottainai Movement.

8. Collection of cleaners wire coat-hangers

A certain company that operates 22 cleaning shops in Kaga City, Ishikawa Prefecture ran a campaign to collect and recycle the wire coat-hangers which used to be thrown away. Also, they had Japan JC's Mottainai Move-ment referred to in the handbill publicizing the coat-hanger recycling.

THE WORLD "MOTTAINAI MOVEMENT" IDEA TREASURE HUNT CONTEST

Under the concept "Let's love all things on earth and make better use of them," we would like to collect treasure in the form of ideas for the "Mottainai Movement."

Instructions: Please write down your ideas for the Mottainai Movement on the individual, family, business or community levels on an application form and send it to your National Secretariat by fax or mail.

Eligibility: All Junior Chamber members and community members all over the world.

Term: From January 1, 1994 to July 31, 1994.

Prize: Individual Grand Prize: air ticket worth US$ 10,000.00

NOM Prize: Memento and plaque will be awarded to the National Organization who collects the most applications.

Should you need details about the application form, please contact you National Secretariat or Japan Junior Chamber.

Figure 12

such as posture and pronunciation, provided the feedback emphasizes the positive not the negative.

The project could be extended through students exchanging ideas and information with other students around the world using email or the Internet.

VARIATION

There are many possible variations depending on the level and age of students. Encourage an advanced class to take notes during the question-and-answer session and use these notes later for a piece of written work, such as a report on the occasion. This project could be undertaken by a whole school, each age level selecting a topic and contributing to a presentation in front of an audience.

COMMENTS

The extent to which this project is conducted in English will depend on your teaching circumstances and the level of your class. Some students may find it difficult to read up background information in English, others may explore a topic in greater depth. Encourage students to work together to translate materials.

Acknowledgements
Many thanks to Bernadette Rodrigues Roselli, Kiddy and Teen English School, São Paolo, Brazil for the original idea.

3 Trips

3.1 Planning a trip

In this project students plan a trip as part of a business English course. This trip can be real or imaginary.

LEVEL	**Elementary to intermediate**
AGE RANGE	**16 years and above**
TIME	**One term** (scheduled at a time when the project can be followed up by the trip, if possible)
GENERAL AIMS	To prepare the class for a trip abroad, or if this is not possible, to plan an imaginary trip.
LANGUAGE AIMS	To use expressions related to asking for information, requesting brochures, etc.; to practise reading skills by accessing the Internet and finding information from library resources; to write emails or letters booking accommodation and flights (for real trips only).
LOCATION	Libraries, tourist offices.
RESOURCES	Maps, brochures, catalogues, underground maps, bus routes, timetables, tourist booklets; information on accommodation and sightseeing attractions; access to computers and the Internet (optional); addresses and phone numbers of tourist-information centres; tape recorders and cameras, video camera.
TEACHER PREPARATION	1 Decide on a destination and dates, then, if you are outside the country of destination, collect the relevant resources.
	2 Make sure that the syllabus includes the relevant areas of travel English and give the students input and practice during the course.
	3 Calculate the approximate cost if you decide to go on a real trip, inform students, and if necessary get parental consent.
STUDENT PREPARATION	If you are already in the country you are going to travel in, students can take responsibility for gathering the resources. They can also search the Internet for useful sites and do general background reading on the country they are visiting.

PROCEDURE

1 In three groups students pool their knowledge of the destination and useful sources of information they have found.

2 Discuss as a class what general and travel topics each group is going to research:

   – *General*: geography, history, education, music, sport, leisure
   – *Travel*: accommodation (A), entertainment (B), transportation (C)

3 After general topics have been chosen or allocated, the groups then do research on these in their own time, building up a file of information, examples, typed-up notes, website printouts, etc. Class time can be allocated for coordinating the material and planning a presentation to the rest of the class.

4 For the travel topics the students work in class as follows:

   – *Group A*: Using the material gathered, students select a number of hotels or bed and breakfast facilities and write letters of enquiry asking for location, availability, prices, etc. These letters/emails should be checked before being sent.
   – *Group B*: Students should write to or phone tourist offices asking for information about museums, galleries, restaurants, shows, sightseeing tours, etc. They should ask about opening and closing times, ticket prices, booking, etc. Any correspondence should be checked before being sent.
   – *Group C*: This group should check the Internet for airline-company sites and on-line ticket sales. They should also contact car-hire and railway companies, check road and rail maps, calculate travel times and costs, the most efficient and convenient means of travelling, etc.

5 One of the most exciting moments in any project is probably when students' letters bring the authentic replies into the classroom. Share all this material by asking students to read it aloud, discuss the information, and note preferences. Put the letters on a notice board in the classroom for everyone to see.

6 When enough information has been gathered, the students then pool their resources. For small classes, this can be done as a class. For larger classes, students should regroup in mixed A, B, C groups. They decide the schedule in detail coordinating all three categories (A, B, and C).

7 The hotel and flights, transfer from the airport to your destination, travel cards, and anything else like theatre or concert tickets, have to be reserved well in advance. For real trips, no bookings should be made without your consent. For imaginary trips, real companies should not be approached for anything more than information.

FOLLOW-UP

The trip itself will involve using English in a wide range of everyday travel situations. The students can video their trip and show it on their return along with a commentary or voice-over. They may also wish to keep a diary, give their personal comments on the trip, give mini presentations based on photos they have taken, etc.

VARIATION

If the class cannot go on the trip, concentrate instead on producing a city fact file which can be made available to others or displayed in the local tourist office for the benefit of potential travellers.

COMMENT

This is a very ambitious project but one which offers a great deal of potential from everyone's point of view.

Acknowledgements
Many thanks to Daniela Calzoni, Istituto Professionale Servizi Commerciale e Turistici, Poppi, Italy for the original idea.

3.2 Climbing Snowdon

This project is unusual in that it has a mountain climb as the end-product! The procedure can be adapted to any location.

LEVEL

Intermediate and above

AGE RANGE

Older adolescent

TIME

15 hours over 3 weeks

GENERAL AIMS

To climb a mountain; to keep a diary of the expedition.

LANGUAGE AIMS

To practise all four language skills; to develop interactive strategies in dealing with peer groups; to keep a written record of the climb.

LOCATION

Any suitable location.

RESOURCES

Maps of the area/mountain; tourist information; Youth Hostel information; car hire (unless your school/college has a minibus of its own); insurance cover for your students; first-aid equipment; camera.

TEACHER PREPARATION

1 Ensure the feasibility of taking your students on an expedition and find out the insurance implications.

2 Contact a guest speaker to talk to students about mountain safety.

STUDENT PREPARATION

Students will spend classroom time (i.e. the 15 hours prior to the actual climb) on a variety of tasks, such as making phone inquiries, writing letters, discussing plans, reading brochures and preparatory information, filling in forms, and listening to a guest speaker.

PROCEDURE

1 Students collect brochures on the proposed expedition from a tourist office or travel agent. It may be necessary for students to make phone calls to these offices if they are planning to travel outside the immediate vicinity. This initial stage also entails detailed planning, scheduling, discussing and negotiating transport, accommodation, food arrangements, sightseeing, and the overall budget for the project.

2 The journey and the actual climb are the central focus of the project. Students need to keep a record or diary of their experiences as a basis for written work when they get back. Encourage them to take photographs to illustrate their presentations (see Figure 13).

3 The final phase of the project involves students writing about their expedition and presenting an illustrated talk to students and teachers from other classes.

FOLLOW-UP

Any aspect of this project could be followed up if it is useful and relevant to your students' needs. In the three weeks' planning beforehand, note any specific language problems that need further work.

VARIATION

This approach to a project can be applied to any excursion, whether it involves a simple one-day excursion or more ambitious travel plans.

COMMENTS

1 A major factor in this project is the financial cost to the individual student. It is essential that everyone is aware of the potential cost before the idea is allowed to develop.

2 If the trip does not take place at a weekend, you also need to consider whether your absence from school will place other colleagues under pressure and whether another member of staff will cover for you.

3 Hiring specialist equipment, like climbing boots, can be expensive, so you should make sure that there are no unforeseen costs to cause embarrassment. Borrow as much equipment as you can.

4 Check that all students are fit enough to undertake anything strenuous, and make sure they are covered by insurance. Obtain parental permission for the trip in writing.

5 One of the best features of this project is the undoubted opportunity it provides for students to build all-round confidence and the comradeship that develops as a result of group bonding.

<u>SNOWDON</u>

INTRODUCTION

This 3-week elective involved the preparation for a weekend in Wales with
the ascent of Snowdon as the highlight, the weekend itself at the end of
Week 2 and a final week of feedback, report writing and settling the
accounts.

PLANNING

All decisions were made by the students and all the preparations were made
by them. This entailed booking accommodation, hiring a car, phoning
equipment-hire shops, working out a route, deciding on food
arrangements,etc. The two teachers, Nicky and I, were only responsible for
the initial idea, for the booking of a talk on first aid by the Red Cross
and for general guidance and encouragement.

Nicky and I shared the elective, dividing our time between the Snowdon
group and the exam elective. This had the advantage that both teachers got
to know the students involved, but it also meant that it was hard to keep a
feeling of continuity from lesson to lesson.

THE TRIP

The trip itself took place over four days. Day 1 and day 4 were travelling
days, day 2 was the climb and day 3 was a visit to Caernarvon and Anglesey.

USEFULNESS FOR ENGLISH

Every stage of the elective involved the use of different language skills.

The planning stage required plenty of <u>speaking</u> in the form of telephoning,
discussion and decision-making, <u>listening</u> to each other, on the phone and
to the Red Cross talk, <u>reading</u> brochures, leaflets, insurance policies,etc.
and <u>writing</u> in the form of letters and forms.

During the trip itself the only language spoken was English and, of course,
the students had the benefit of two English teachers constantly 'on call'
to help with language problems. The local people spoke mainly Welsh, which
was interesting (though not particularly useful for listening practice!)
but they were all bi-lingual so the students had plenty of opportunity to
practise their English in cafes, shops, the Youth Hostel, etc.

The feedback stage involved further discussion and report writing and
students will have useful practice at speaking in public when they make
their Snowdon presentation to the rest of the school.

HIGHLIGHTS

Speaking personally, the highlight of the trip was undoubtedly the shower I
had after arriving back in the youth hostel following the climb!

Another thing that sticks in my mind is the fear of being on top of Snowdon
in a snowstorm, our route back down the mountain becoming harder and harder
to find as the mist grew thicker and the path became covered in snow. The
courage of my companions, Mayumi and Nathalie, impressed me greatly and the
determination of all the group to get to the top was impressive too.

Another highlight was the guided tour of Caernarvon Castle. Our guide was
clearly fascinated by history and enjoyed bringing it alive for other
people.

Figure 13

I also remember being impressed by the powers of organisation of all the students, but especially Yusaku, and by the wonderful team spirit that developed. In fact, the biggest problem at the youth hostel was to <u>stop</u> everyone helping with the washing up because the kitchen wasn't big enough!

RECOMMENDATIONS FOR THE FUTURE

The idea of using <u>cars rather than a minibus</u> was a good one because it made the journey faster safer and less tiring. The only problem was that it split the group in two but we always met up for refreshment stops.

The <u>hiring of equipment</u> needs to be more efficient. Mayumi worked very hard on the telephone but perhaps she should have had more guidance from the teachers. We wasted several hours on Day 2 getting the equipment. We now know that youth hostels sometimes hire out equipment very cheaply but they don't necessarily have a lot of choice. There is also a company in Cottenham (near Girton) which hires out equipment and this needs investigating.

The blizzard we met at the top of Snowdon was a surprise even for the experienced climbers in the group. We must make sure that everyone realises that <u>these mountains can be really dangerous at any time of the year</u> because of the unreliability of British weather.

In order to avoid the embarrassment and worry caused by Daniele dropping out at the last minute, we should insist on everyone paying a deposit of, say, £20 at the beginning of the planning stage. This might make students more aware of their responsibility to the group.

FINAL COMMENTS

The trip had many <u>positive aspects</u> which I would like to stress in this final section:-

confidence building   ("I <u>can</u> speak on the phone")
sense of achievement   ("We did it. We climbed the highest mountain in
                          England and Wales")
group feeling   (meeting at Halfway House on the way down)

English   ("I spoke English all weekend")

life experience   (I, for one, will never forget struggling down the
                          mountain in a snowstorm)
FUN   Claudia's card game, now called Chilean Snap!

Acknowledgements
Many thanks to Sheila Levy, Cambridge Academy of English, Cambridge, England for the original idea.

3.3 The zoo

This project involves completing a questionnaire during a visit to a zoo. The language needed is rehearsed beforehand by using a dummy questionnaire for classroom practice.

LEVEL	**Elementary to lower–intermediate**
AGE RANGE	**Young adolescent**
TIME	**5 lessons, followed by whole day spent at the zoo**
GENERAL AIMS	To produce a report or wall display on the trip to the zoo.
LANGUAGE AIMS	To enable students to describe and talk about animals; to practise and use the present simple and continuous tenses.
LOCATION	Classroom, followed by trip to the zoo.
RESOURCES	Simplified maps of the zoo, so that students are able to find their way around; camera (optional).

TEACHER PREPARATION

1 Before the project, obtain a fact sheet from the zoo so you know what it has to offer. If the zoo provides educational packs for school visits you could exploit this to stimulate student interest (see Figure 14 for sample worksheet). You may need to prepare a 'dummy' questionnaire (see 'Procedure', stage 2) for practice purposes.

2 Check the cost of a group visit and buy/book the tickets before the visit. Unless your school is funding the trip, make sure that students' parents/guardians are prepared to pay the transport and zoo entry costs. You may also need to look into insurance cover for the day trip.

STUDENT PREPARATION

Students bring photos or pictures of their favourite animals to class, think about the animals they would like to see when they visit the zoo, and look up the English words for these animals before the lesson.

PROCEDURE

1 The initial stage of this project focuses on covering the vocabulary students need in order to talk about animals, what they eat, which countries they come from, and the kind of habitat they live in. Students may come up with names of animals which may not be in the zoo, but at this brainstorming stage of the project that does not matter.

The ZOO Project

Name: ....   Class: ....
....   Date: ....

Hello and welcome to the ZOO!! Answer all the following questions, please.
Use <u>sentences</u>, not only words.

What is the first animal that you can see ?
....

<u>Are there any gorillas? How many?</u>
....

What is the baby monkey doing now?
....

How many girraffes can you see?
....

Where are the kangaroos from?
....

Which animal is next to the tigers?
....

Which animal is between the emus and the zebras?
....

Which animals can you feed? (Give 3 examples.)
....

What is the "surname" of the dog?
....

<u>Are there any baby-animals? Give examples.</u>
....

Which of the birds is the biggest?
....

What do the elephants eat?
....

<u>Which animals do not live in the cage? Give four examples.</u>
....

<u>Which animals can swim in a pool or a "lake" ? Give two examples.</u>
....

<u>Which animals are from Africa? Give five examples.</u>
....

<u>Can you see any snakes or crocodiles? If yes, give two names of them.</u>
....

<u>* Choose one animal and describe it - minimum ten, maximum twenty
sentences.</u>

* What is the name of the animal? * What colour is it? * Where is it from? * What does (not) it eat?
* Are you afraid of it? *Why? * Can you have it at home? *What is the animal doing now? ....

....
....
....
....
....
....
....
....

And now, the EXTRA question for you:
   Which animal do you like the best? Why??

....
....
....

And .... that is ALL !! Thank you for your hard work !!

Your English Teachers

Figure 14

Encourage students to contribute to the topic in as many ways as possible. They may wish to share contributions about favourite animals, mascots, toy animals, and story-books and films featuring animals.

2 Students work in pairs on the next stage, practising the language they need to use in order to complete the worksheets. The content of the worksheet will vary depending on what you decided to include. If you want students to practise present simple and continuous tenses within the zoo topic, use material which is not part of the final worksheet. Construct a short dummy questionnaire which familiarizes students with the target grammar.

3 Students work together on the dummy questionnaire, either inventing answers or using whatever input material you have provided.

4 Monitor their work and make a note of any problems which need to be followed up. Get students to hand in their questionnaires so you can check their work.

5 On the day of the zoo visit, give out the worksheets once you have arrived and not before.

FOLLOW-UP

If you want to extend the topic, this visit offers many possibilities. Students can write a short report of their visit, either individually or in pairs, focusing on the past tense. Use any photographs taken during the visit for a wall display using captions and added drawings.

VARIATION 1

If the project generates a lot of detail, students may be interested in putting together an information pack in English for the zoo. They can use the existing pack from the zoo as a model. To make the end-product as useful as possible, check with the zoo in advance that the pack will be welcome and invite suggestions on what else could be included.

VARIATION 2

This project works equally well with different venues, such as a museum or art gallery.

COMMENTS

1 Don't allow the preparatory language focus to become too prominent at this level, so that the real activity remains fresh and stimulating and students can feel relaxed about the task and enjoy their visit.

2 There is often some cultural sensitivity to the environmental and ethical issues involved in the existence of zoos, circuses, safari parks, saving rare species, etc. This project provides an opportunity for students to discuss such issues constructively.

Acknowledgements
Many thanks to Ludmila Balikova, Olomouc, Czech Republic for the original idea.

4 Local

4.1 Local fashion

In this project students produce a guide to local fashion outlets for customers and visitors.

LEVEL	**Upper-intermediate and above**
AGE RANGE	**Older adolescent and above**
TIME	**2 weeks**
GENERAL AIMS	To do research and conduct a survey based on a questionnaire about local fashion retail outlets, resulting in a guide for visitors.
LANGUAGE AIMS	To use the following: question forms; formal and informal register; countable and uncountable nouns; expressions of quantity, such as *a few*, *most*, *the majority*, *a minority*, etc.
LOCATION	The local shopping area.
RESOURCES	Clipboards; paper; a computer, a printer, a photocopier; card for front cover (optional); a camera and film (optional).
TEACHER PREPARATION	1 Check that the students are interested in the topic. 2 Check access to a local shopping area which has a number of fashion outlets. 3 Ask for permission from parents and from colleagues if the students may miss other classes.
STUDENT PREPARATION	Think about what information visitors might wish to get from the guide.
PROCEDURE	1 Explain the project, and as a class, make a list of fashion outlets in your area. Brainstorm what should be included in the guide. You may wish to include some of the following:

- hours and days of business
- location and access
- type of outlet (shop, department store, market stall, etc.)
- price range
- type of fashion, range of goods
- quality of goods, service, premises
- value for money
- overall rating.

2 In pairs or small groups the students prepare a questionnaire to get answers related to the above. Pool their questions and ideas on the board. When the class has prepared enough questions, ask for volunteers to produce a clean word-processed version that can be photocopied. Do a final edit before copies are made.

3 Establish the opening lines which will be used when approaching people on the street and shop staff. Hand out clipboards and copies of the questionnaire. Students role-play interviews using the questionnaire. Check for fluency and accuracy and the use of the anticipated language.

4 Confirm which outlets the students are going to visit and get permission from the manager/person in charge for your students to visit, talk to their staff, and take photos (if this option is taken up). For street interviews, decide on the best locations. Make sure that students have some identity badges showing who they are and which school they come from. Put students into pairs and agree on a finishing time and a place to meet. Make sure they have the school phone number and some change/a phone card in case they get lost.

5 As a group, go to the agreed locations and conduct the survey. Monitor the students and help with any problems.

6 Once enough information and opinions have been gathered— this may take several outings—the students come back to the school, get into groups, and process the results.

7 Discuss with the class how they think their findings should be presented. Make sure that they have access to a computer, printer, and photocopier. If photos have been taken, have them developed. They can be photocopied along with the students' text. In groups, students produce their guides.

8 The guides should then be distributed to other students, teachers, the school library, etc.

FOLLOW-UP

Depending on the results of your monitoring, you may wish to review the use of the targeted language.

VARIATION 1

This project could also be done in a non-English speaking country. In this case, the answers to the questionnaire will need to be translated.

VARIATION 2

The project could also be done with younger, intermediate learners. In this case, you may wish to do more language practice in class before the survey.

VARIATION 3

Guides could also be produced for other kinds of outlets, services, or facilities, for example, sports/fitness centres, hospitals/clinics, etc.

COMMENTS

Speaking and listening skills are crucial to the success of the interviews, and students are more likely to realize their own strengths and weaknesses once they have actually encountered the authentic experience of using the language outside the classroom.

Acknowledgements
Many thanks to Jane Barnes, Bell School of Languages, Saffron Walden, Essex, England for the original idea.

4.2 Visit your teacher's house

In this project students organize a visit to their teacher's house and video or photograph it.

LEVEL

Elementary

AGE RANGE

Adult

TIME

10 lessons plus 1 morning for visit

GENERAL AIMS

To give students a clear focus for their work; to produce and learn to edit a video as part of the end-of-course entertainment.

LANGUAGE AIMS

To revise vocabulary and structures covered in the previous weeks of the course.

LOCATION

Teacher's home.

RESOURCES

Clipboards for worksheets; computers, scanner; access to an editing suite; video camera; music CDs and CD player.

TEACHER PREPARATION

1 Prepare worksheets in advance so that your students have a focus during their visit (see Figure 15 for sample). Build into the worksheet any vocabulary and structures you want to revise and allow some space for students to write their own questions. The worksheet should be clearly set out with plenty of space for students to write down the information they gather.

2 Arrange transport, either by booking your school minibus or using public transport. If your students offer to use their own cars, check on the insurance implications. Check also on the insurance provisions for visits outside the school.

3 Ask students what they would like to eat and drink during their visit and look into the costs involved and who is going to buy everything. If your school does not have a budget for this kind of event, discuss with your students whether they are prepared to share the costs.

Your teacher's house

Before you visit your teacher's house think about these things.

A. What do you think the house will be like inside and outside?

B. Will there be a garden? What do you think you'll be able to see in the garden?

C. How many rooms do you think the house will have?

D. List five things you think you will see in

the kitchen

the living room

the dining room

the bathroom

E. What colour do you think the rooms will be? White or another colour?

Visiting your teacher's house:

A colour Quiz

Your teacher will tell you which rooms you can look in. Then find one object for each of the colours listed below.

Blue	gold
Green	silver
Yellow	purple
Pink	brown
Red	black
White	grey
Orange	cream

A-Z of your teacher's house

Your teacher will tell you which rooms you can look in. Then find one object for each letter of the alphabet.

A		N	
B		O	
C		P	
D		Q	
E		R	
F		S	
G		T	
H		U	
I		V	
J		W	
K		X	
L		Y	
M		Z	

users/outhere/stafhous
17/11/98 DC

Figure 15

STUDENT PREPARATION

Students bring in photos of their own homes if they wish.

PROCEDURE

1 Initiate a class discussion on homes and houses. Ask students to talk about their own homes. Some students may have photos of where they live which they can bring to the next lesson. If there are different nationalities in your class, ask students to describe their homes. At this level you may have to feed in some vocabulary for various kinds of houses, for example, *detached*, *semi-detached*, *terraced house*, but as this project is designed for the end of the course, you will know what vocabulary your students have covered by then.

2 The next stage of the project is the visit to your home. Prior to this, students will each have a worksheet which you can give them in advance or leave to the morning of the actual visit. When they complete the worksheet, ask them to record their impressions.

3 During the visit students will video or photograph your home, the various rooms, and any special features which spark their spontaneous interest. Try to ensure that everyone gets a turn using the camera and that as many students as possible feature in the film.

4 Students write up an account of their visit. Depending on the facilities available, these accounts can be written on a computer with some of the video pictures scanned in or handwritten using photographs (see 'Variation').

If you are working on video in an editing suite, students need to watch the footage and write an accompanying storyboard, i.e. what is on the video. They then select clips and edit the video accordingly.

It is unlikely you will have a soundtrack, unless you have the luxury of lapel microphones, in which case your students will have to write their own captions and subtitles to accompany what people are going to watch. As well as the written captions, your students can add their own choice of music to liven up the sound effects.

5 The video can be shown to other classes or the whole school at the end of the course.

FOLLOW-UP

Give students a follow-up worksheet which asks them to record how their expectations were met (or not) during the filming.

VARIATION 1

Vary the start of this project by asking students to contribute articles from newspapers or magazines about people's homes. Ask them to collect advertisements from estate agents or to download examples from the Internet. If they do not know where you live, they could speculate about the kind of home you have and how it is furnished.

VARIATION 2

If you don't have access to all the technical equipment, this project works perfectly well using a Polaroid/instamatic camera. Allow students to work on their written accounts in small groups so that the photographs can be shared out.

COMMENTS

1 This project can be adapted for different levels, in which case the worksheets could be devised in conjunction with students. They can speculate on what they might or might not find in your home. The more advanced and mature the group, the more likely it is that students will work independently. In small groups they can write worksheets which they exchange before the visit, so that each group has a task set by another group.

2 Some students may feel quite shy about being in their teacher's house, but getting them to prepare food and drink is usually a good way of encouraging a more relaxed atmosphere.

3 The size of your class has quite a bearing on this project, not only in terms of the number of students you want in your home and how many students can effectively work on one film in one editing suite, but also in terms of cost and making multiple video copies.

4 You can find a more detailed discussion of this particular project in the ARELS magazine *Arena* Feb/Mar 1999.

Acknowledgements
Many thanks to Denise Clenton, Cambridge Academy of English, Cambridge, England for the original idea.

4.3 Home sweet home

In this project students conduct a survey of UK and local property.

LEVEL

Elementary and above

AGE RANGE

Adult

TIME

2 hours a week over 3–4 weeks

GENERAL AIMS

To produce a display of housing images and charts designed to compare the local and UK housing markets by interviewing local English-speaking residents and looking at websites and newspapers.

LANGUAGE AIMS

To activate the language learned in the classroom; to increase students' awareness of spoken English by exposing them to natural native-speaker English including features such as accents and the use of conversational fillers; to make comparisons.

LOCATION	Estate agents, local native English-speaking residences (optional).

RESOURCES — Clipboards and tape recorders for conducting interviews; cameras (optional).

TEACHER PREPARATION

1 Gather information on the British housing market by calling estate agents, browsing their websites, or by reading property newspapers and magazines. Make sure you have photographs of various kinds of housing in the UK.

2 Establish that there are British residents or visitors in your area who are willing to be interviewed and set up interviews in advance of the project.

3 Make sure your students are familiar with the vocabulary of buildings and housing, and that they already know how to use the simple present tense and question forms.

STUDENT PREPARATION — Students need to collect information about their local property market.

PROCEDURE

1 Students rehearse the language needed to interview people through role-play and questionnaires.

2 As a group, discuss the fundamental differences in house design and the different connotations certain words may have – as this project was originally done in Spain, it was relevant to discuss words such as *bungalow* and *villa*.

3 Sort out all the material so that the information can be categorized under various headings such as: location—town/country; design—modern/period; price—cheap/expensive; furnished or unfurnished; for rent or to buy, etc.

4 Design an 'Estate Agent's Window' display of a wide variety of properties with their various descriptions.

5 Students interview British residents and visitors about their homes abroad and in the UK and talk about their 'ideal' home. If practical, the interviewees can be invited to the school, as opposed to being interviewed in their homes.

6 Students draw graphs and pie charts to illustrate the following comparisons between their own country and the UK:

 – the popularity of various kinds of property
 – the proportion of home ownership to rented property
 – the ages at which people leave home to buy or rent property
 – the difference in housing prices.

FOLLOW-UP — This topic leads to the financial and legal aspects of home-buying and is invariably of interest to students both personally and professionally. It provides plenty of practice in the uses of *have to*, *can/can't*, and *do/don't*. As a follow-up, this particular group of students also produced a *Buyer's Guide for British People in Spain*. This additional end-product provided a step-by-step guide from first viewing to completion of purchase.

VARIATION 1

Students working on this project were elementary level language learners and worked mainly in legal, financial, or property services. However, this project would obviously work well with more advanced students who, as the topic is of interest to most people, would not necessarily need to come from a business background.

VARIATION 2

The approach and organization of this project would lend itself to other subjects such as cars, restaurants, furniture, etc.

VARIATION 3

The *Buyer's Guide* could form part of a longer project and the end-product could meet a genuine need, if appropriate.

COMMENTS

Students initially found the use of tape recorders rather inhibiting but ultimately the recordings were very useful. Undertaking a project at such an early stage in their learning meant that students were apprehensive about tackling interviews. However, by keeping closely to the questionnaire format and discovering that people quite happily responded to requests to speak more slowly and repeat their answers, students' self-confidence was greatly enhanced.

Acknowledgements
Many thanks to Jackie Martin, The Victoria English Centre, Torrevieja, Spain for the original idea.

4.4 My homeland, my hometown

This project is designed as a guide for English-speaking visitors to your students' hometown. It provides a choice of end-product, and the focus can cover your students' town/city, region/province, or the whole country.

LEVEL

Elementary and above

AGE RANGE

Adolescent

TIME

8 lessons (but very flexible)

GENERAL AIMS

To create an end-product to be used by visitors or tourists to students' town, area, or country; to foster self-confidence and self-esteem through working independently.

LANGUAGE AIMS

To practise all four skills through researching, questioning and interviewing, telephoning, writing, etc.

LOCATION	Classroom, libraries, tourist and information offices, bus and train stations.
RESOURCES	White and coloured card/paper; glue, felt-tip pens, markers, scissors; access to word-processing facilities (optional); cameras; postcards, magazine and/or newspaper cuttings; maps and other tourist information; cassette recorders (optional).

TEACHER PREPARATION

1 Any project involving work outside the classroom requires forward planning and organization. Younger students should always work in pairs or small groups, and you will need parental and head teacher/director permission for students to work outside the classroom.

2 Collect some or all of the reference material yourself for initial discussion purposes, or invite an outsider (a foreign resident, for example) to come and talk about his/her hometown/country. Use the Internet to find sample material, download it, and use it to stimulate student interest and act as a model for their own work.

3 Unless the resources mentioned are available, you will need a small budget to purchase extra materials.

STUDENT PREPARATION

Students need to be thoroughly familiar with the area they are intending to write about. Although information will be available from libraries and tourist information offices, students need to visit places in their own vicinity to check facts, take photographs, or make drawings.

Ask students to bring in material such as maps and pictures. If you anticipate a short project, rely on students to collect material in advance. In a longer project collecting information can create some of the momentum and build up students' interest and group commitment.

PROCEDURE

1 Students work in small groups to decide on the focus of their project (town, region, or country) and the kind of end-product they want to create. They should consider what they would want to show a foreign visitor.

Their choices dictate whether they need to visit libraries and town archives or interview local people or tourists for extra background information.

2 Make sure you agree clear deadlines so that everyone knows how long they have to collect their realia and prepare their end-product.

3 Students start collecting their information. Encourage them to consult you and discuss with each other in English. Monitor what is going on and consolidate new vocabulary and structures by using the 'Language monitor' (see page 16).

4 The final stage involves developing the end-product. If groups are preparing maps, they will need time to draw pictographs and stick pictures onto their outline map. The map also needs a key explaining the pictographs. Point out that brochures, leaflets, and guides need photos and illustrations, and these will need to be collected and collated. Students with IT skills can devise and design the leaflets/brochures, using computers to enhance their artwork.

5 When students have collated all their material they exhibit and share the result with other groups in the class and with other classes in the school if possible.

FOLLOW-UP

The potential for follow-up work is wide-ranging. There are many opportunities to practise the language needed to interview people in the street and to transcribe the interviews.

If the class has produced a single large wall map, this can be exploited for teaching purposes, such as giving directions, locating points of interest, describing routes, etc. Students could also write letters to penfriends suggesting a holiday tour based on the leaflet or information sheet which they have been involved in preparing.

VARIATION 1

Younger students might be motivated to work on an end-product based on an imaginary city or country.

VARIATION 2

More advanced students could be asked to produce a guidebook on a city which none of them has visited but have researched and which could be used as a basis for a proposed visit.

VARIATION 3

Individual students can use their own tourist guide to conduct the rest of the class around the various sights in their town, while the other students could play the different roles of interested, bored, absent-minded, or know-it-all tourists. This activity could be videoed for future analysis with students.

COMMENTS

If your students envisage producing material to distribute for tourists for actual use, this will require multiple copies and cost money which you are unlikely to recoup. Consider approaching the town's tourist office to see whether the officials would be willing to display some of your students' work so that visitors can benefit from up-to-date information and enjoy the fact that it has been produced by local students.

Acknowledgements
Many thanks to Janna Sikorova, Zakladni Skola, Novy Jicin, Czech Republic, and Zofia Soltys, Elementary School No. 34, Warsaw, Poland for the original idea.

4.5 Food and drink labels worldwide

In this project students collect labels from food and drink items from various countries and give a presentation based on their findings.

LEVEL	**Elementary and above**
AGE RANGE	**10 years and above**
TIME	**3–4 × 45-minute lessons**
GENERAL AIMS	To produce a wall map displaying links between food and drink labels and the country of origin; to give a presentation based on this display.
LANGUAGE AIMS	To use vocabulary related to the names of countries, and food and drink items; to use the structures: *comes from, is produced in, produces.*
LOCATION	Students' homes, dormitories, school kitchens, waste-disposal areas.
RESOURCES	Large sheets of stiff paper or card; atlases; coloured felt-tip pens, pins, thread.
TEACHER PREPARATION	You need to set up this project well in advance so that students have time to collect as many food and drink labels or wrappings as possible from cartons, tins, packets, jars, and bottles. Provide a large box for students to put their contributions in, and encourage competition by noting and praising those students who are really making an effort. You can withhold what you are planning to do with all the labels, if you think mystery adds to motivation!
STUDENT PREPARATION	To collect as many labels, wrappings, and cartons as possible.

PROCEDURE

1 Depending on the amount of material collected and the size of your class, put all the labels on to a central table and ask students to make a list of all the different countries where the food and drink has been produced.

2 Ask students to locate the countries in an atlas.

3 Put students into small groups and allocate countries to each group. Students go through the material, picking out items from their countries and making a list of the products.

4 The next stage is to produce a large world map with a wide border. Students attach the labels of their products to this border as near as possible to the countries the products come

from. They then link the labels to the countries with pins and thread—preferably colour-coded.

5 Each group then prepares an oral presentation summarizing their findings. They should include any trends they find, such as: *Our country produces a lot of fruit products.*

FOLLOW-UP

Students can write a report on their findings.

VARIATION

Students could also visit local supermarkets and shops and research where items come from, each group looking at different categories, for example fruit, vegetables, canned food, and toiletries. Ask the manager of the shop for permission before you go!

COMMENTS

This project is very easy to set up, but make sure you start with a sufficient supply of labels, wrappers, etc. The project could be done at beginner level if the presentation stage is simplified and more teacher support is given.

This project was devised by the author.

4.6 The wheelchair-friendly guide

In this project students produce a guide for disabled people in the town where they are studying.

LEVEL

Upper-intermediate and above

AGE RANGE

16 years and above

TIME

40 hours over 12 weeks

GENERAL AIMS

To produce a fact sheet for disabled people on the facilities for wheelchair users; to make the information available on a school/college website (optional).

LANGUAGE AIMS

To practise all four language skills; to use the language of introductions; use of formal and polite language, question forms, and thanking.

LOCATION

Public facilities, shops, cinemas, other public places.

RESOURCES

Notebooks or clipboards; storage facilities (see page 14); a large sheet of paper or thin card; a large town/city map; camera or video recorder (optional); computer with facilities to create a website or web page; cardboard, stapler, plain paper; a word processor or typewriter and printer or photocopier; a wheelchair (if possible on loan for the duration of the project—optional).

TEACHER PREPARATION

1 You should arrange for a small budget to cover bus fares, phone calls, entrance fees (if necessary), petrol if you intend using your own car.

2 Make sure that your students are sufficiently interested and willing to give up their spare time, and are aware of the extra commitment this kind of project requires. You will need permission from your head teacher, your colleagues, and the parents or guardians of your students, if they are not adults.

3 Each student will need an identity card (see page 14) and you should arrange for the loan of a wheelchair.

4 If you can arrange for an outside speaker who is a wheelchair user and willing to talk to students about the topic, this is a very positive way to sensitize students to the topic. If possible, use a classroom with easy outside access and ideally one which you can use after school hours.

5 You could check if any of your students have direct personal experience of being involved with disability as their contributions may be of great value in the initial discussions.

STUDENT PREPARATION

If you have a wheelchair, students (or those who want to do so) could practise using the wheelchair. If this is to be done off school premises, check that your students are covered by insurance. The best place to practise is a park or recreation area.

PROCEDURE

1 Students work in pairs and brainstorm the target areas. Some examples are:

– hotels, bed and breakfasts, restaurants, bars, cafés
– public transport: buses, trains, taxis, stations
– museums, art galleries
– banks, shops and shopping malls, public toilets
– theatres, cinemas, amusement arcades, discos
– sports centres
– doctors, dentists
– schools, colleges, universities
– tourist attractions.

2 Students then divide up the list and plan where they will visit and when, possibly after school hours. The use of the wheelchair has to be coordinated by all the pairs.

3 The schedule should be put up on a large grid on the classroom wall. Figure 16 gives an example of what this grid might look like.

4 Students prepare questions for their research trips. Input the target-language items and practise them through role-plays until students are reasonably confident. They should also be prepared for unpredictable responses.

5 Students take it in turns to use the wheelchair, if possible, or carry out the work on foot, phone for information, and check

SAMPLE GRID

Students	Week 1 11–12 noon	Week 2 3–4 p.m.	Week 3 7–8 p.m.	Week 4 11–12 noon
Victoria and Claire	6 banks in High Street W/C	Check hotel lift doors— widths	Check as many restaurants as possible	Visit sports centre
Sophie and Guy	Station— on foot	3 museums W/C	Check as many restaurants as possible	Check shop doorways
Regula and Thorleif	See City Architect to discuss developments for disabled	Phone bed and breakfast to check facilities	Try three cinemas W/C	Take photos of 'hopeless' and 'ideal' places
Tassy and Yuko	Check pavement heights in city centre	Interview taxi drivers	Try two theatres W/C	Check public toilets W/C

All meet at café at 8 p.m.

Figure 16

the facilities. Students can take photographs of good practice—a ramp leading into a bank—or bad practice—revolving doors into a museum. This will generate material for the language follow-up.

6 Set aside a time each week for students to give progress reports and review the research done.

7 When all the locations have been covered, the pairs write up their research, preferably on a word processor to an agreed format which is clear and accessible. The accuracy of the information should be confirmed.

8 When all the students' work has been collated, it can be made into a booklet using double-sided folded sheets.

FOLLOW-UP

This stage depends on the end-product and the kind of exposure the group decides on. The booklets can be distributed by students to relevant and interested organizations: tourist offices, local magazines, newspapers, radio or television stations.

Students studying abroad can contact their own countries and send copies of the project (in their mother tongue) for publication at home. The class may want to discuss their findings, show photos they took, and send requests to any locations with poor facilities.

VARIATION 1

The final product could be a website, if you have the facilities: a computer with web-production software, a digital camera, or a scanner if photographs have been taken with a 35-mm or Polaroid camera.

VARIATION 2

The idea could be also used to produce a guide for parents with small children. The problems of access for wheelchairs are similar to those for prams and pushchairs. In this case, students can research establishments which cater sympathetically for small children: shops, cafés, department stores with changing/feeding facilities; restaurants with children's menus, high chairs, toys; towns which provide supervised and sometimes free play areas for parents to leave their children for a couple of hours; easy parking spaces for parents with pushchairs, and so on.

COMMENT

This project can do a lot of good for the community and be very satisfying for your students.

This project was devised by the author.

4.7 English is everywhere

In this project students choose an end-product using language they have identified in the course of collecting realia.

LEVEL

Elementary

AGE RANGE

Adolescent

TIME

3 lessons, one week apart

GENERAL AIMS

To foster cooperative learning and learner independence; to create an end-product using student findings, for example designs for a T-shirt, fridge magnet, schoolbag, or pencil case, sticker for a mobile phone, wrapper for an ice lolly or chocolate bar, etc.

LANGUAGE AIMS

To develop learners' ability to identify and learn new vocabulary; to expand students' awareness of how much English vocabulary there is around them.

LOCATION	Classroom and shopping centres, supermarkets, news stands after school hours.
RESOURCES	Clipboards for written records are useful if the information cannot be taken away; large sheets of cardboard/paper, coloured felt-tip pens, glue, scissors.

TEACHER PREPARATION

1 Before the project, tell students to collect samples of realia with English words. They need enough material for each group of four to have a range of ideas to draw on.

2 As students will be collecting information outside school hours, alert parents to this fact well in advance.

STUDENT PREPARATION

Students collect as many different examples as possible of magazine pages, newspaper articles, advertisements, package wrappings, labels, and other realia with English words on them.

PROCEDURE

1 Students work in groups of four to plan the project. They choose their own area of research to find out how much English is used in daily life. Suitable areas for investigation are likely to include fashion and clothing, supermarket food and drink products, computer language, company names, magazine titles, local shop names, instructions included with electrical equipment such as televisions and CD players, and language associated with sport (for example, in football— *corner*, *dribble*, *penalty*).

2 Make sure each group has a clearly defined topic and, if necessary, suggest that one member in each group takes responsibility for checking that everyone knows what they are expected to contribute. At this stage, students decide on their end-product. Each group decides whether they all make an oral contribution to some aspect of what they have found out, or whether one person acts as the presenter for the whole group.

3 The end-product preparation can be done in class or in students' own time, depending on the time available. If students are working in their own time, check that their work will be ready in time for the lesson scheduled for presentation to the rest of the class.

4 Students present their designs. After they have been discussed in class, display the end-products either on the classroom walls or somewhere central as a focus of interest for other students.

FOLLOW-UP

If this project can be done at the beginning of the school year, it provides a stimulus for learning vocabulary, as students can see the relevance of learning new words. You will certainly find ways of exploiting the vocabulary on the designs during the course of your lessons.

VARIATION

Although this project is geared to elementary students, a similar approach can be used with intermediate students on a shorter time-scale so that the work is more concentrated.

COMMENTS

1 Students who initially seem reluctant to participate quickly realize how much English there is around them and how accessible the language is.

2 If there is one really effective and popular design, for example, a sticker for a mobile phone, such as *Ring me now. I'm waiting for your call!*, students could make the sticker and put it on their mobiles.

3 The content of this project is entirely student-led and open-ended, so you cannot predict what words students will come across. When students come to listen to each presentation they are not likely to remember all the new vocabulary, so it is important to make sure that the designs are displayed in the classroom and that students can study the words at leisure.

Acknowledgements
Many thanks to Regina B. Gomes, Escola Municipal Sakura, Teresopolis, Brazil for the original idea.

5 Classroom

5.1 Valentine cards

In this project students learn about the tradition of St Valentine's Day and design a card.

LEVEL	Elementary
AGE RANGE	Adolescent
TIME	**Approximately 2 hours**
GENERAL AIMS	To make Valentine cards.
LANGUAGE AIMS	To practise writing skills.
LOCATION	Classroom.
RESOURCES	Coloured card or stiff paper, crayons, paints, felt-tip pens, glue; computer-artwork facilities (optional).
TEACHER PREPARATION	Collect or prepare some examples of Valentine cards (optional).
STUDENT PREPARATION	Ask students to find out the kind of symbols, motifs, and language associated with Valentine cards.
PROCEDURE	1 Introduce the topic and check that students know the date (14 February), and the tradition (cards are sent anonymously to the object of someone's affections).
	2 Have a look at some examples and highlight the kind of messages sent and typical design features (hearts, cupids, pink, etc.; see Figure 17).
	3 Put students into pairs and distribute the materials. Ask them to design a blueprint for a card on paper first, decide on a suitable message, then design their cards.
	4 If you have a mixed-gender class, some students may wish to have their cards 'delivered'. You could act as a discreet post person. The cards are posted to you with instructions only you can see. You then deliver the cards. Students can try to guess who the cards came from.
FOLLOW-UP	Students can write cards to students in other classes who can reciprocate if they wish.

Figure 17

| VARIATION | This project lends itself to other occasions in the English calendar, such as Christmas, Easter, and on a more informal basis, birthday, congratulations, and good-luck cards. |

COMMENTS

Choose to do a project like this so that it coincides with the appropriate month in the year!

Acknowledgements

Many thanks to Zsuzsanna Nagyne, Szombath Tagiskola, Pécs Egyetem, Hungary for the original idea.

5.2 Showtime!

In this project students produce and perform a voice-over for an extract from a film.

LEVEL

False-beginner

AGE RANGE

Older adolescent

TIME

About 6 lessons

GENERAL AIMS

To perform a dubbed clip from a movie; to get students talking in English.

LANGUAGE AIMS

To practise storytelling; to practise translating from native language into English; to practise writing skills; to practise pronunciation (optional).

LOCATION

The classroom or audio-visual room, students' homes.

RESOURCES

Television and video recorder. Preferably the students should have access to these both inside and outside class.

TEACHER PREPARATION

1 You need to provide students with a worksheet setting out the guidelines for the project.

2 Make sure that whichever film a group chooses, the video of that movie is available for classroom use. Check whether the students have access to a television and video recorder outside class.

STUDENT PREPARATION

None.

PROCEDURE

1 Divide your class into small groups, four to five in each group, and tell your students to choose a movie in their mother tongue that they all really enjoy.

2 On a worksheet tell them to list the major stars and the director, to describe the storyline (the plot), and to identify what they think the message of the film is, if it has one.

3 They then need to choose a clip from the film (about 5 minutes long) which shows interesting character interaction, transcribe it into their mother tongue, and then translate it into English. This may be done during class time or during the students' free time. It might be necessary to vary the group sizes in order to cater for the number of characters who appear in each clip.

4 Check the translation for any major grammatical errors and then each member of the group chooses one of the roles.

5 Each group rehearses their speaking roles against the film clip with the sound turned off. Once again, you need to monitor and support individual pronunciation if necessary, although this should not become burdensome and you should allow for the fact that the students are building other things into their performances.

6 After sufficient practice, each group presents their film clip to the class by initially providing background information and plot, followed by playing out their 5-minute performance.

FOLLOW-UP

The project could be followed up with work on aspects of pronunciation/intonation, word/sentence stress, production of individual sounds, etc.

VARIATION 1

A multilingual class of students can follow up this project with English-language films, provided that you know they are accessible on video. The translation stage of the project is not likely to be needed.

VARIATION 2

An advanced group of students can carry out this project by being as creative as they like, incorporating background music and sound effects to enhance their performance.

VARIATION 3

Encourage students to use animated or cartoon films which provide greater opportunities to explore character voices for a really convincing final performance.

COMMENTS

1 Make sure that all the groups have a chance to perform in front of the class.

2 Be alert to the possibility that strong students may carry weaker ones along in the course of this project, as so much of the practice takes place outside the classroom. However, this is one of the strengths of project work and there are reciprocal benefits in terms of sharing and confidence building.

3 This project is particularly suited to false beginners, especially if they have followed a language course which has focused on grammar and translation. Shy students can shine because they take on the role of someone else. Those who lack confidence are motivated by employing the familiar skills of translating from their mother tongue and the project offers scope for writing and speaking skills.

Acknowledgements
Many thanks to Barbara J. Wells, Soka Women's College, Tokyo, Japan for the original idea.

5.3 Quiz contest

In this project students produce their own quiz series about British culture and topical news.

LEVEL	**Upper-intermediate and above**
AGE RANGE	**Adult**
TIME	**2–3 months**
GENERAL AIMS	To help improve students' understanding of British culture through researching, compiling, and doing a quiz contest.
LANGUAGE AIMS	To practise all four language skills; to practise writing, specifically note-taking; to practise the use of question forms; the accurate use of grammar.
LOCATION	Library.
RESOURCES	Encyclopedias, library reference section, newspapers and news programmes, magazines; a scoreboard; blank cards; video camera and monitor (optional), video recorder; video of British television-quiz programmes; access to the Internet.
TEACHER PREPARATION	1 Check students have access to a variety of the above resources including, if possible, useful website addresses. Prepare some examples of quiz questions in categories such as general culture, recent general news, recent sports news, recent entertainment news, etc. aimed at the level of the class. 2 Prepare video clips of quiz contests from British television, such as *Who Wants to be a Millionaire?*, *Weakest Link*, *University Challenge*, etc. (optional). For UK-based teachers only—take students to a pub quiz.
STUDENT PREPARATION	All students should do background reading and research on British culture, and watch or listen to news programmes.
PROCEDURE	1 Show the class examples of quiz programmes and explain they are going to create a quiz contest. Ask the class to brainstorm the kind of questions that are asked in a television or pub quiz and write their suggestions on the board. Topics could include: history, the arts (literature, music, art), geography, everyday culture, famous people, domestic news, pop music, sport, films and television, etc.

2 Ask the class some of the questions you have prepared. Highlight the forms that quiz questions take and quiz show protocol – examples of these can be taken from the video clips. Picture and sound questions are also welcome. These can be taken from the radio, television, EFL textbooks, etc.

3 Put the class into two groups. One group writes the questions and answers, the other group 'produces' the quiz, provides entertainment between the rounds, the quiz master, the scorer, and so on. Tell the first group to decide on their categories and allocate categories to members of the group. Students should do research on their areas between lessons or, if time and resources are available, they can prepare during class time. The second group should plan the staging, layout, and timing of the contest and think of some entertainment, for example, a television commercial break. See Figure 18.

4 The questions should be short, have a clear, objective answer, and be pitched at the right level. You should ask a group to rewrite any questions that you consider too difficult. The questions should be written on card with the answers on the back.

5 When each team has compiled 40 questions, set up the classroom with two groups facing each other. If you have a video camera, make sure it is set it up so that all the participants fit into the picture. When everything is ready, the quiz can begin.

6 Depending on students' enthusiasm, you can hold a quiz regularly during the term. You should rotate students so that everyone has a chance to be in the quiz and production groups.

FOLLOW-UP

If you video each contest, you can check students' use of language, weak areas, etc. You can also highlight the funny or exciting parts to show to the class as a whole. At this level, encourage students to self-assess, perhaps focusing on a different aspect of speaking skills each week, such as stress, rhythm, and intonation one week or pronunciation the next. The writing of questions is also an opportunity for checking grammatical accuracy.

VARIATION

The idea for this project lends itself to any topic, length, or format depending on how long you want to devote to it. In adapting it to a lower level you would have to ensure that the questions were well within students' capabilities so that the contest was a positive experience! The contest can extend to other classes in your school of the same level.

COMMENTS

The teacher who devised this project records that students found it a very satisfying and worthwhile experience with

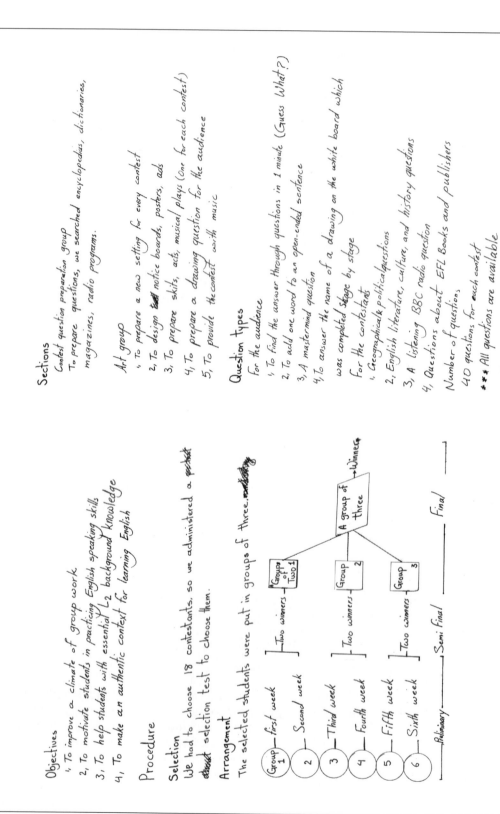

Figure 18

everyone feeling really motivated to use the language. This particular project involved 170 students from a number of classes and took about five months.

Acknowledgements
Many thanks to Mehdi Dedebeigi, English Department, University of Tabriz, Iran for the original idea.

5.4 The island

This project allows students to follow the procedure stages flexibly, omitting stages as they wish. The development of an imaginary island scenario can be as simple or as detailed as your students want to make it.

LEVEL	**Elementary to intermediate**
AGE RANGE	**Adolescent**
TIME	**Open-ended (see 'Comments')**
GENERAL AIMS	To produce an exhibition portfolio of work based on students' lives on an imaginary, uninhabited island.
LANGUAGE AIMS	To extend topic-specific vocabulary; to practise first-conditional sentences.
LOCATION	Classroom.
RESOURCES	Video camera and/or a tape recorder (optional); television and video recorder; coloured paper.
TEACHER PREPARATION	Depending on your approach to this project, pre-teach new vocabulary at the beginning of each lesson, or elicit the vocabulary needed from students and allow them to develop the opening scenario.
STUDENT PREPARATION	None.
PROCEDURE	1 Set up this project by presenting the class with a scenario. For example, the class has won a competition and the prize is a trip to a mystery location. Or they have won the lottery and decide to go on holiday, but the plane has to make an emergency landing and they all find themselves on an uninhabited island. (If you choose to base the project on the latter scenario, ensure that students are not going to find it disturbing.)

2 Once students have chosen their scenario, they work individually or in small groups to create simple cartoon strips showing how they come to be on the island.

3 Ask students to draw a map of their island on a large sheet of card which can be displayed later. They can make individual maps, or you can give each group a large sheet and allow individuals to work on different parts of the map. They next draw a key, using symbols for the various features and the kind of vegetation on the island, for example, mountain, rock, forest, wood, waterfall, lake, brook, canyon, swamp, deserted village, cave, marsh, quicksand, volcano— the list will depend on students' contributions. Various features can be named, for example, *Shark Point, Deadman's Swamp,* etc. Use pictures from magazines or flashcards if you need to stimulate their imaginations.

4 Students decide on what they will need in order to survive. They might have emergency kits with them or you can supply a list of what is available.

5 They then build a home, which they have to design using materials available on the island. They also have to decide what kind of tools they will need and how they will manage. Where will they build their home? High up so a passing ship might see them? Near fresh water or a source of food? What about hygiene facilities? Students draw and label plans for their home.

6 Students design clothing to wear, also using materials found on the island, and then draw and label the items.

7 Students next agree on the rules needed for everyone to get along together and decide how to deal with infringements of the rules.

8 They discuss what they would miss most from their old life.

9 Students design a flag for their island. Explain the symbolism of certain flags and elicit the significance of colours. For example, on the Thai flag, blue is for royalty, white for monks, and red for the people. Students decide on appropriate colours, shapes, and symbols.

10 Students invent or adapt some games to keep themselves amused on the island. For example, noughts and crosses in the sand, solitaire with pebbles, or they may come up with an entirely new game based on the island.

11 Students plan an escape or a rescue bid. Do they want to escape? How will they do it? Would they rather wait to be rescued?

12 At the end, students return back home and are interviewed on their experiences. Who is there to meet them when they get back? Family, friends, the media? Will they miss anything about the island? Are they all pleased to be back? How will

the experience affect them in the future? You could film or record these interviews. Doing so will also give you a chance to see how much new language is being recycled.

FOLLOW-UP

The follow-up activities depend on the initial activities and your students' enthusiasm for the central idea. There is a great deal of scope involving the four language skills, especially writing skills, if your students choose to:

– develop an island newspaper, using photos, pictures, and drawings to illustrate the articles
– describe an island adventure, either using their diary or writing within a word frame which you supply—they could explore the island, climb a mountain, encounter a monster, etc, and these accounts can be adapted and incorporated into the island newspaper at a later date
– write a postcard home, to be sent as a message in a bottle or attached to a bird's leg
– create a tourist brochure for the island, advertising its attractions. They can describe its geographical features, food, things to do, accommodation, etc. They can also consider the implications, financial and environmental, if the island is developed for tourism.

VARIATION 1

A young class might enjoy making a model of the island using papier mâché, clay, plasticine, or any other materials available. They could use a cardboard box or a sand tray and 'plant' trees, using a mirror for a lake, for example.

VARIATION 2

Younger students can invent some fantasy animals for their island. Fold a piece of paper into three, draw a head on it and pass it on for the next person to draw a body, who then passes it on for the legs to be drawn. The animals can be coloured and labelled. It may be necessary to teach new vocabulary or for students to look up words for things like *scales*, *tusks*, *claws*, *humps*, etc. The animals can be given names and students can discuss what the animals eat, their habitat, their characteristics and then write this information in the form of a factsheet.

Students can also make mobiles or three-dimensional models of the different animals.

VARIATION 3

An advanced class could keep a diary describing how they feel on the island, what they see, the events of the first day and how they reacted, etc. This will involve students using language to describe moods, feelings, and reactions. A lower-level class can use a cartoon strip to illustrate how they feel.

COMMENTS

1 This project can encompass a couple of one-off lessons or take a whole academic year to complete. As most of the activities are self-contained, you can choose to conclude the

project at any stage, without leaving students feeling that it is incomplete. As some students work more quickly than others, you can choose to reserve some of the activities as extension activities, since it does not really matter whether the whole class covers all the tasks. You could even select certain topics for certain groups and use the end-product for display purposes so they can all see each group's work. Each group can be assigned a colour and their work can be colour-coded. If this project is going to extend over a few months it will then be easier to locate and keep each group's work together.

2 The language arising out of this project depends on the activities you choose. For example, if you want to include stage 4, your students will need to use simple conditional structures like: *We'll need a knife if we want to cut down the bamboo.* You can introduce these structures or give further practice if they already know them.

Acknowledgements
Many thanks to Clare Handysides, Assumption Thonburi College, Bangkok, Thailand for the original idea.

5.5 Pocket-money survey

This project motivates teenagers as it focuses on them and their lifestyles. It can also be adapted for adult classes.

LEVEL	**Intermediate**
AGE RANGE	**Adolescent (can be adapted for adults)**
TIME	**Approximately 6 lessons**
GENERAL AIMS	To research and report on teenage spending habits, with a choice of end-product.
LANGUAGE AIMS	To practise question forms and the language of comparison and contrast.
LOCATION	The interviews based on students' questionnaires are conducted outside the classroom. If you want to avoid this, arrange for students to carry out their interviews with other classes provided your colleagues agree.
RESOURCES	Clipboards for each group; paper or card for a large graph or block diagram; materials for an illustrated group report; IT facilities, etc.
TEACHER PREPARATION	Find newspaper or magazine articles about teenage spending in other countries.

STUDENT PREPARATION

None.

PROCEDURE

1 Draw students' attention to what teenagers in other countries spend their money on. You might talk about the cost of designer jeans/trainers or approach the topic by displaying a poster featuring poverty or malnutrition as a way of introducing/contrasting lifestyles.

2 Once the idea has generated some class discussion, students work in pairs or small groups. Ask them to suggest topics and questions to discuss. For example, they could research the spending habits of their own year, of students in years above or below them, what their parents or grandparents used to spend their pocket money on, etc.

Some students may supplement their pocket money with part-time jobs after school or at the weekend and this factor may need to be included in the questionnaire.

Allow groups with different ideas to pursue these. Depending on students' suggestions, there could be the potential for projects comparing different generations' spending habits, for example.

3 Students write and design their own questionnaires, using IT facilities if available. Figure 19 shows one way of organizing a simple questionnaire.

ITEM	AMOUNT (per week)	NAME
Mobile phone	£5, £14, £2	Maria, Dieter, Yoko
Magazines		
CDs		
Sport		
Entertainment (cinema, clubs, etc.)		
Clothes		
Savings		
Others		

Figure 19

4 When students have agreed on what questions they want to ask, make sure they can ask the questions fluently. If necessary, set up a brief role-play session so that they are confident in handling the questions.

5 Make sure the copies of the questionnaires are printed, photocopied, or handwritten before you and your students agree on the time they will need to interview as many people as possible. Keep to a short schedule, or the project will lose momentum and completed questionnaires get lost.

6 Keep to the schedule you have agreed, so that the next lesson focuses on collating all the information students have collected. If all students have used the same questionnaire, allow class time for a general feedback session. If different questionnaires have been used, each group of students can present a brief report on their results. This stage allows you to exploit the findings orally, and also alerts you to the kind of language needing further input before students prepare their reports, summaries, charts, etc.

If the project is a whole-class project, students need to agree on dividing up responsibilities for who produces text, artwork, diagrams, etc. Pairs or small groups generally work more quickly.

7 Ensure that students have completed their end-product(s) and then display them. Invite other classes in to see the exhibition and discuss the findings with your class.

FOLLOW-UP

The information can be presented as a formal report, as a summary of findings, or as a subjective piece of individual writing. The topic also develops students' awareness of paragraph linking, as each category of spending forms a separate paragraph.

VARIATION 1

This approach can be used with adult learners to investigate personal budgets. However, since many people would not want to reveal their earnings, tell students to set one imaginary salary figure for everyone in the class. Students can then retain the way they prioritize their spending, so that the relative distribution of income and expenditure is genuine. The categories could include: rent/mortgage, food, transport, clothes, entertainment, mobile phone, newspapers, services (gas/electricity/water/oil, etc.), and whatever else students themselves suggest.

VARIATION 2

With an older group of students who are aware of global issues and inequities in distribution of wealth, the project could be further developed to focus on the contrast between the cost of designer labels and the wages paid to the workers in the countries where the clothes are made, as well as the workers' working conditions.

COMMENTS

If you are teaching a class with students from low income families, the topic of real pocket money could be insensitive. In this case, ask students to develop the idea along the lines of *How much pocket money would you like to have? What would spend your money on?*

This project was devised by the author.

5.6 Would you like a cup of tea?

This is a short, carefully controlled project which consolidates the structures and vocabulary of giving and carrying out instructions.

LEVEL

Elementary

AGE RANGE

Any age

TIME

2 × 45-minute lessons

GENERAL AIMS

To familiarize students with a British custom; to produce an instruction page for a student magazine; to enable students to create their own presentation based on giving instructions (optional).

LANGUAGE AIMS

To encourage giving and listening to instructions; to practise the imperative.

LOCATION

Classroom.

RESOURCES

Collect things you need to make tea: a kettle, water, tea, sugar, milk, biscuits, tablecloths, teapots, milk jugs, sugar bowls, paper serviettes or kitchen paper, and a cup and saucer and a teaspoon for each student; white and coloured card for vocabulary cards; video camera (optional).

TEACHER PREPARATION

1 Make small vocabulary cards with the names of the various things (teaspoon, milk jug, etc.) that will be on the tables. Use white card for the objects and coloured card for the verbs (*prepare, boil, put, pour, steep, stir, brew, add*). Each group needs its own set of cards. If you want the materials to last, it is best to laminate them.

2 To prepare and motivate students before the project, ask them to look for any kind of tea produced by UK companies, either by looking in local shops or at home, and to bring the full/empty packet/box to the first lesson.

3 Try to collect pictures illustrating the history of tea.

STUDENT PREPARATION

Look for tea produced by UK companies. Suggest how the classroom furniture could be rearranged to look like an English teashop, and find supporting illustrations.

PROCEDURE

1 Put students in groups of four. Tell them to lay the tables/desks leaving one desk for the kettle. Encourage students to talk for a few minutes about what they like and dislike drinking at different times of day.

2 Start the discussion on the different teas students have brought. Ask:

   – *What can you learn about the tea from the packet?*
   – *Where does the tea originally come from?*
   – *Can you guess how many cups of tea the average Briton drinks a day?*

   You may also have additional information or pictures about the history of tea that you want to introduce into the discussion.

3 Give students the white vocabulary cards with the names of the objects and ask them to match what is on the table with the words. Encourage students to work together as a group so your intervention is minimal. When everything has been correctly matched, ask them to say the words, and then put the cards in a column on the board.

4 Students watch as you mime making a cup of tea. Repeat the same sequence, but this time say what you are doing.

5 Distribute the verb cards and ask students to match these cards with the ones you have already put on the board. There will now be two columns of words on the board to use for giving instructions. Prompt the structure by holding up an object, for example, a kettle, and saying *What do we do with this? We boil water in a kettle.*

6 When you are satisfied that the language has been practised sufficiently, model making tea so students can start making their own. Begin by miming what you are doing, and then use the imperative form of the verbs to describe what to do. Give the instructions slowly, step by step, and let students make tea in small groups.

7 Try to spend a few minutes with each group as they drink their tea and eat their biscuits, and ask them to describe the process of making tea.

FOLLOW-UP

Recycle the oral language in writing by asking students to produce an instruction page for a student magazine. Students can work in pairs or do the work at home individually. Depending on their age, students could produce illustrated and labelled instructions and display them around the classroom.

Further follow-up could involve students working in pairs to produce the same instructions for a television programme. If you have the facilities, video their presentations for feedback. This gives students the opportunity to analyze and discuss their work.

VARIATION

This approach can be applied to any topic which involves giving and following instructions, for example, making a kite or a mask, or cooking different food. In a mixed-nationality class you could demonstrate something typically English, an apple tart, for example. Students use this as a model for developing a project based one of their own national dishes.

COMMENTS

This project builds on earlier versions of similar projects carried out by Belgian and Finnish teachers (see first edition, pages 16, 83–4).

Acknowledgements
Many thanks to Janna Sikorova, Zakladni Skola, Novy Jicin, Czech Republic for the original idea.

5.7 Board game

In this project students produce board games based on one or more different countries.

LEVEL

Elementary to intermediate

AGE RANGE

Any age

TIME

3–4 lessons over 1 week

GENERAL AIMS

To design a ready-to-use board game about a country.

LANGUAGE AIMS

To practise simple present tenses (elementary); past and future tenses, simple, continuous, and imperative forms (intermediate).

LOCATION

Classroom, library, travel agent, tourist office (optional).

RESOURCES

Blank maps of selected country with a few details marked on it, for example, a map of Australia showing gold mines or a map of Poland showing haunted castles; coloured card; small buttons or tokens to represent the players.

TEACHER PREPARATION

1 The games involve pairs of students writing down instructions for a route through a country, which then has to be followed by another pair of students. So familiarize yourself with a chosen country by reading background information. If you choose Australia, for example, you will need to know about the main tourist attractions, the outback, the Aborigines, etc.

2 Prepare blank maps for the country you chose, one for each pair of students.

3 Pre-teach the language of games, such as *Miss two turns. Go back. Move to number 12. It's your turn*, etc.

STUDENT PREPARATION   None.

PROCEDURE

1 Give students their maps and ask them to predict what they are going to do with them. In this way you can elicit the aim of the project.

2 Tell the class something about the country you have chosen. Elicit any information students may already have about it.

3 Working in pairs, students pick a starting point on their map, from which they draw a route. As they draw their route through the country from one geographic or cultural feature to another, they write down sentences describing adventures and hazards they encounter on the way. Each adventure needs to be numbered.

4 Ask students to correct each other's sentences or correct them yourself.

5 Students rewrite the corrected sentences on separate pieces of card and then illustrate and colour the blank maps in any way they wish.

6 The finished games can then be exchanged between pairs. Students take it in turns to read the sentences and follow the instructions taking them along the route. Students can judge the effectiveness of the sentences they are given by the success with which they are able to trace the routes.

FOLLOW-UP   Students can use their journey and its accompanying adventures as the basis for a written narrative or story.

VARIATION 1   Students do their own research on various countries in small groups. They share this information with other groups and then decide which country or countries to use. Groups can swap their maps and base their game on another group's map. This exchange motivates students to produce more challenging maps!

VARIATION 2   This project provides an excellent opportunity for cross-curricular studies and building on what students know from their other studies in history and geography. The project can be adapted to form a very sophisticated project focusing on geographical features such as rivers, mountains, national parks, etc. For this variation, liaison with teaching colleagues is essential. If information and resources can be shared it may also reduce your initial preparation time.

COMMENTS	1 Younger students have to be encouraged to believe they are capable of writing their own sentences. Once they have produced a game and it has been played they are proud of the achievement.

2 Some students may need hints on how to incorporate 'short cuts' into their route, for example, *You find a small boat so you row across the river.* Each map will be different, so no two games will ever be the same.

Acknowledgements
Many thanks to Zofia Soltys at Elementary School No. 34, Warsaw, Poland for the original idea.

5.8 Famous foreign cities

This project is designed for students to research a particular foreign city and to create a large illustrated wall map. The project can also provide cross-curricular links with their history and geography studies.

LEVEL	**Any level**

AGE RANGE	**Any age**

TIME	**Approximately 6 lessons**

GENERAL AIMS	To produce a wall display or fact sheet about a foreign city; to encourage confidence and increase understanding of foreign countries.

LANGUAGE AIMS	To practise all four language skills in addition to developing dictionary skills needed for translation.

LOCATION	Classroom.

RESOURCES	Large sheets of card/paper, coloured pens, glue, scissors; access to videos, CD-ROMs, feature films, etc.

TEACHER PREPARATION	1 Negotiate with your students which city you will work on. Collect as much realia as you can about the chosen city, such as leaflets, tickets, receipts, postcards, etc. The *National Geographic Magazine* is an excellent source of pictures and information.

2 Talk with the geography and history teachers about the city, and download city maps, pictures, and text from the Internet.

3 Prepare a short talk to introduce the city and capture your students' imagination. Include something anecdotal or legendary for interest.

4 Establish whether there is a source of tourist video material available. At the end of the project it might be fun to show students a video of their chosen city.

STUDENT PREPARATION

Students collect as much information as possible about their city in English and in their mother tongue.

PROCEDURE

1 Give your short prepared presentation on the foreign city and then pool all the materials that have been collected.

2 Encourage pairs/small groups of students to choose places in the city that interest them, for example, the Eiffel Tower or the Arc de Triomphe in Paris, and to read about them.

3 Each group looks at the detailed information they have collected and decides how they are going to present it.

4 Monitor what is going on and tell each group they will have a fixed amount of time to present their findings to the rest of the class.

5 Draw a large blank map of the city on the board. Each group talks about the city, sharing information they have gathered. Put the name of each place mentioned on the board in its correct geographical location in the city. That way you build up a city map so your students can go on an imaginary city tour.

6 Students work on producing the largest possible wall map. Each group may need to work on a different section of the map. Transfer the names and places from the board to the final wall map, as near as possible to the actual location.

7 Tell students to write up the accompanying texts and to put these up beside the relevant sites. They can illustrate the map with tickets (for the Eiffel Tower, for example), and pictures or photos from leaflets to make one huge map collage.

FOLLOW-UP

The map can later be used for practising the language of description, past tenses based on a visit to the city, future simple tenses for travelling, prepositions of place, etc.

VARIATION

More advanced students can look at certain places in more depth. A group researching Washington DC, for example, can research the Capitol in detail.

Acknowledgements
Many thanks to Zofia Soltys at Elementary School No. 34, Warsaw, Poland for the original idea.

5.9 Internet exploration

This project uses the Internet as a basis for student presentations on places or topics of their choice.

LEVEL	Intermediate
AGE RANGE	Any age
TIME	3–4 hours (very flexible)
GENERAL AIMS	To work on collaboration and negotiation skills with a partner; to develop cultural awareness of a specific country; to create end-products in the form of posters, brochures, fact sheets, leaflets, web pages, video documentary, or illustrated talks to the class.
LANGUAGE AIMS	To practise and improve intensive and extensive reading skills. There is likely to be a wide range of unpredictable new language arising as students download information. Focus on the language students will need for their presentations, otherwise the material could turn into a reading comprehension exercise!
LOCATION	Students need access to the Internet.
RESOURCES	Ideally each student or pair of students needs to use a computer with Internet access. If the number of computers is limited, students take it in turns to use them and work on other parts of their project in the meantime; tape recorders and video camera (optional).

TEACHER PREPARATION

1 If your students have not used the Internet before, you will need to arrange for technical support, unless you are able to handle this yourself.

2 If you think your students will not be able to name any specific towns or cities of interest to them, produce a list of possible places with one or two facts designed to encourage further interest.

3 Prepare a back-up set of instructions, a simple instruction sheet (see Figure 20 for a sample), and a stock of reference materials—maps, brochures, etc.—in case of technical failure of the equipment.

STUDENT PREPARATION

None, but ask students to try and gain some experience of using the Internet in advance of the project.

PROCEDURE

1 Outline the purpose of the project and tell students they can choose how to present their findings to the rest of the class.

2 Students work in pairs and discuss with each other whether there is a particular place they would like to know more about. If they cannot think of anywhere, supply them with your prepared list. Each pair must choose a different place, preferably somewhere they are genuinely interested in finding out more about.

3 Students use the Internet in pairs to find out as much as possible about their chosen place. Ensure that one of each pair has IT skills and suggest a time limit on this activity. Students use the various search facilities to scan-read texts, pictures, maps, etc., and to download any information that looks potentially useful for more intensive reading at a later stage. Encourage students to rely on their own scanning abilities for contextual and visual clues in the first instance, using dictionaries only as a last resort.

4 Students decide how they will present their information. Their choice will depend largely on the time and resources available and how much information they have collected. Some students may need more help than others in designing their end-product so you should be available as a facilitator/motivator to ensure that students do not lose momentum once they have collected sufficient information.

5 Students present and exhibit their end-products to the rest of the class.

Oxford Tourist Information Office

Congratulations!

You have been offered a job at the tourist office in Oxford.

Visitors are going to ask you information, so prepare yourself.

Look at this website: http://uk.yahoo.com

Find information about:

> ➤ the history of the town
> ➤ the monuments and museums in the town
> ➤ events and activities in the town
> ➤ hotels, bed and breakfast etc

Good luck!

Figure 20

FOLLOW-UP	The project lends itself to a variety of follow-up activities. Involve other classes/students in an interactive display at the presentation stage. Pairs of students listen to each other and take notes on what they hear. They then in turn present the information to another pair of students.
	The project can be further exploited for discussion, debate, or a written report using all the contributions, to study the differences/similarities between the various towns and cities.
VARIATION 1	This project can be adapted for lower-level groups. Ask students to search for specific information on cinemas, restaurants, hotels, pop music, theatres, theme parks in different towns. Use the information to practise the language of comparison.
VARIATION 2	Ask more advanced-level students to search for information to help them to compare political systems in a number of different countries.

Acknowledgements
Many thanks to Helen Wright, Heathfield School, Ascot, Berkshire, England for the original idea.

5.10 Creating a book advertisement

This project uses the works of Agatha Christie to develop reading skills and generate an end-product to advertise her books.

LEVEL	**Upper-intermediate**
AGE RANGE	**Older adolescent**
TIME	**7–10 hours**
GENERAL AIMS	To familiarize students with the works of Agatha Christie; to develop students' ability to identify and focus on the main ideas in a book; to stimulate purposeful reading and research; to encourage students' creativity and ability to work independently; to produce a book advertisement in the form of a wall poster.
LANGUAGE AIMS	To read a number of novels by Agatha Christie; to identify the language of persuasion as used in advertisements; to look at the language of translation if books are not in English; to make an oral presentation in English.
LOCATION	Classroom and library.
RESOURCES	A number of books by Agatha Christie, not necessarily in English; paper or card for posters; coloured felt-tip pens.

TEACHER PREPARATION

1 Ensure enough of the chosen author's best-known books are available. You will also need to collect some background information about the author before embarking on this project.

2 Find some examples of book advertisements. Give them to students either at the start of the project, or after they have tried writing their own advertisements.

STUDENT PREPARATION

Before the project begins, students need to do some background reading in order to discuss and decide which book will be the focus of their advertising project. Initially they can work in pairs in the library and/or the classroom reading through the books available. They should not read the books in detail. Tell them to look through the texts and to read the publisher's blurb and the introductory chapters or preface in order to get an idea of what the book is about.

PROCEDURE

1 Divide the class into groups of about five or six. Students tell their group what they have found out, negotiate which book to choose, and discuss possible ways of advertising it. The content of the advertisement should reflect the theme of the book.

2 Students use their shared ideas and suggestions to draft an advertisement, using one of the models you provided earlier. As you monitor what each group is doing, encourage students to focus on what makes an effective advertisement.

3 In addition to the text, which they write in English, students also need to think about how to make the advertisement visually eye-catching.

4 The groups assemble their text and illustrations to make the wall posters.

5 When the posters are completed, each group briefly tells the rest of the class something about the book they are advertising, using their poster as a visual aid.

FOLLOW-UP

If the presentations have been successful in your own class, your students might wish to advertise their books to other classes and perhaps act out a scene from it for their own class or others. Depending on what they decide, they may then need to consider whether or not to use music and what kinds of costume and props are necessary. Two or more groups could work together if one book or scene is very popular. Students will have to assign roles, organize costumes, props, music, furniture, and rehearse their scene so that they can perform in front of the whole class.

VARIATION 1

This project can also be used to look at other kinds of products and the language used to advertise them. Ask students to carry out their own research into other areas, such as the language used to advertise holidays, by researching Internet, newspaper, television, high-street, and travel-shop marketing campaigns.

This project can be adapted to many other topics, for example, to a piece of music, a picture or painting, a television programme, a poem, a film, etc. The project is also adaptable to different ability levels and the time allowed for the end-product presentations can be adjusted accordingly.

VARIATION 2

If students become very well-informed about a particular subject, you might like to organize a quiz, game, or competition and award a small prize to the team which scores highest.

COMMENTS

Some students initially found this project rather daunting because they had to skim through unfamiliar books. However, the teacher's enthusiasm for Agatha Christie enabled her to sell the idea to her students.

Acknowledgements
Many thanks to Yevgeniya Rudich, English Specialized School No. 3, Kharkiv, Ukraine for the original idea.

5.11 Horror stories

In this project students explore and reproduce the horror-story genre in their own writing, with a choice of end-product.

LEVEL

Upper-intermediate

AGE RANGE

Adolescent

TIME

At least one hour a day over two weeks

GENERAL AIMS

To familiarize students with the English horror-story genre; to encourage students to practise the genre in their own writing; to give students an opportunity to work independently and as part of a team to encourage their self-esteem; to produce a class reader, a story for a website, or a wall newspaper based on horror stories.

LANGUAGE AIMS

To develop vocabulary and work on tenses, sentence and paragraph linking, and adjectival word order.

LOCATION

Classroom and library.

RESOURCES

Magazines to cut up as a picture resource; brushes, paints, and drawing materials to create own illustrations; video camera (optional); horror-story video (optional).

If you intend to produce a class reader, you will need word-processing facilities and stiff card for the cover.

If you want to put the end-product on the Internet, you will need access to the school/college website.

TEACHER PREPARATION

1 Before the project, choose a classic horror story at the appropriate level and check that your school library/ English language department has it. Ensure you have enough copies for your class.

2 If you have a horror story on video, make sure the content is appropriate. If the class has been studying the genre in their literature lessons, students will already be familiar with different examples.

STUDENT PREPARATION

Students collect old magazines for later in the project. In their own time, they read at least one horror story to set the scene and provide sufficient information for them to contribute to class discussion.

PROCEDURE

1 Students work in small groups, taking it in turns to talk about the stories they have read. During this exchange, they should discuss some of the elements common to horror stories: characterization, atmosphere, suspense, fear, and scene or context. As each group contributes ideas, list them so that everyone can discuss what makes an effective horror story.

2 Decide on the end-product(s). Depending on the resources available, different groups could contribute to a class reader, others could produce a wall newspaper.

3 Students work on their own horror stories. This may be quite challenging for some students, so allow them to work together if they wish. Another approach is for the whole class to devise a plot and for each group to write their own chapter. This requires more liaison and discussion between groups to make sure the chapters hang together. Encourage students to keep to deadlines and impose a maximum word length, bearing in mind the aims these stories are intended to achieve.

4 For presentation purposes, students type up their stories, using a word processor if possible.

5 Students work on the design and final layout by including illustrations for the story. If they are working on a wall newspaper, they need to write/include advertisements, quizzes, crosswords, agony columns, readers' letters—even stormy, doom-laden weather forecasts—providing everything is relevant to the theme!

FOLLOW-UP

If facilities allow, produce other class readers and bind them in a stiff cover to survive frequent thumbing!

Display the wall newspaper(s) where other classes can read them. Place a box where other students can leave their responses, opinions, or comments on the content to provide feedback for your students.

Organize a competition for other students to submit horror stories to be read and judged by your own class. Offer the winner(s) a small prize.

Students can consider dramatizing one of the more successful horror stories, which would require them to script the story. This could be extended by recording it (with all the sound effects) or even filming it.

VARIATION

This project works with other topics such as customs and traditions, clothes and fashions, hobbies, etc.

COMMENTS

When this kind of project links in with another subject, such as literature, history, or geography, there is a valuable cross-curriculum benefit for both teachers and students.

Acknowledgements
Many thanks to Yevgeniya Rudich, English Specialized School No. 3, Kharkiv, Ukraine for the original idea.

Appendix

Useful websites

It is possible to access a wide range of information by using these directories and search engines.

Yahoo – *http://www.yahoo.com*

Type in a word, e.g. 'rainforests' and *Yahoo* will show the categories under which 'rainforests' is listed and then give a list of websites. Alternatively, you can click a category box on the home page and the directory will supply a list of suggestions.

Google – *http://google.com*

altavista – *http://www.altavista.com*

Type in a keyword and these search engines will give a list of all the web sites which contain reference to that word.

Ask Jeeves – *http://www.ask.com*

This site will answer questions on topics you are interested in or suggest popular websites.

Search Engine Watch – *http://searchenginewatch.com*

This site contains useful tips about using search engines and gives web searching tips.

Bibliography

Brusch, W. 1991. 'The role of reading in foreign language acquisition'. *ELTJ* 45/2.

Describes the setting up of an experimental reading project in Germany involving the provision of class libraries in fifteen schools in Hamburg.

Hedge, T. 1993. 'Key concepts in EFL: Project work'. *ELTJ* 47/3.

A short article which focuses on the definition and role of project work in educational thinking.

Kershaw, G. 1993. Language programs in development projects. Asian Institute of Technology, Bangkok, Thailand, AIT RELC Conference.

Task-based learning in the form of project work based in Papua New Guinea. The discussion includes reference to four kinds of authenticity: learner input, task, event, and learner experience.

Mackay, R., S. Wellesley, and **E. Bazer.** 1995. 'Participatory evaluation' *ELTJ* 49/4.

Focuses on a case study in Indonesia, which describes how the concept of systematic evaluation of teaching activities was introduced to teachers and managers in a language teaching project.

North, S. 1990. 'Resource materials for library project work'. *ELTJ* 44/3.

A versatile, real-life way to replicate many features of a normal library; develops the idea of a 'mini-library' which can be used as a resource base to support different approaches to project work; draws on experience of work done with students in Beijing, China.

Skehan, P. 1998. *A Cognitive Approach to Language Learning,* Oxford: Oxford University Press.

An applied linguistics book which discusses psycholinguistic and cognitive aspects of language learning, taking account of individual learner styles and the role of project work as a vehicle for equipping learners for autonomy.

Stephenson, H. 1993. 'Management and participation in ELT projects'. *ELTJ* 48/3.

Discusses ELT projects and development aid with a view to introducing new practice for ELT practitioners.

Vincent, S. 1989. 'Motivating the advanced learner in developing writing skills: A project'. *ELTJ* 44/4.

A project carried out in Poland involving official letter-writing, followed by a visit to Shell Offices in Warsaw. Exploits *Shell World* and details follow-up in terms of articles for publication, etc.

Williams, M. and **R. Burden.** 1993. 'The role of evaluation in ELT project design'. *ELTJ* 48/1.

An article describing the process of evaluation of a sheltered immersion project at a bilingual school in Geneva, Switzerland. It reflects the fears of some teachers when faced with innovation and how teachers saw shared project work as one of the ways to greater bilingualism and breaking down cultural barriers.

Yule G. and **W. Gregory.** 1987. 'Survey interviews for interactive language learning'. *ELTJ* 43/2.

A paper which discusses the constraining effect of a teacher on a class. A good argument for developing social interaction outside the classroom when training graduate assistants from different nationalities.

Other titles in the Resource Books for Teachers series

Beginners, by Peter Grundy—communicative activities for both absolute and 'false' beginners, including those who do not know the Roman alphabet. All ages. (ISBN 0 19 437200 6)

Class Readers, by Jean Greenwood—activities to develop extensive and intensive reading skills, plus listening and speaking tasks. All ages. (ISBN 0 19 437103 4)

Classroom Dynamics, by Jill Hadfield—helps teachers maintain a good working relationship with their classes, and so promote effective learning. Teenagers and adults. (ISBN 0 19 437147 6)

Conversation, by Rob Nolasco and Lois Arthur—over 80 activities to develop students' ability to speak confidently and fluently. Teenagers and adults. (ISBN 0 19 437096 8)

Creating Stories with Children, by Andrew Wright—encourages creativity, confidence, and fluency and accuracy in spoken and written English. Age 7–14. (ISBN 0 19 437204 9)

Cultural Awareness, by Barry Tomalin and Susan Stempleski—challenges stereotypes, using cultural issues as a rich resource for language practice. Teenagers and adults. (ISBN 0 19 437194 8)

Dictionaries, by Jonathan Wright—ideas for making more effective use of dictionaries in class. Teenagers and adults. (ISBN 019 437219 7)

Drama, by Charlyn Wessels—creative and enjoyable activities using drama to teach spoken communication skills and literature. Teenagers and adults. (ISBN 0 19 437097 6)

Drama with Children, by Sarah Phillips—practical ideas to develop speaking skills, self-confidence, imagination, and creativity. Age 6–12. (ISBN 0 19 437220 0)

Exam Classes, by Peter May—preparation for a wide variety of public examinations, including most of the main American and British exams. Teenagers and adults. (ISBN 0 19 437208 1)

Film, by Susan Stempleski and Barry Tomalin—ideas on how to integrate film into a general course and how to set up film projects, and a glossary of useful terms. (ISBN 0 19 437231 6)

Games for Children, by Gordon Lewis with Günther Bedson—an exciting collection of games for children aged 4 to 12. (ISBN 0 19 437224 3)

Grammar Dictation, by Ruth Wajnryb—the 'dictogloss' technique—improves understanding and use of grammar by reconstructing texts. Teenagers and adults. (ISBN 0 19 437004 6)

The Internet, by Scott Windeatt, David Hardisty, and David Eastment—motivates learners and brings a wealth of material into the classroom. For all levels of expertise. Teenagers and adults. (ISBN 0 19 437223 5)

Learner-based Teaching, by Colin Campbell and Hanna Kryszewska—unlocks the wealth of knowledge that learners bring to the classroom. All ages. (ISBN 0 19 437163 8)

Letters, by Nicky Burbidge, Peta Gray, Sheila Levy, and Mario Rinvolucri—using letters and e-mail for language and cultural study. Teenagers and adults. (ISBN 0 19 442149 X)

Listening, by Goodith White—advice and ideas for encouraging learners to become 'active listeners'. Teenagers and adults. (ISBN 0 19 437216 2)

Literature, by Alan Maley and Alan Duff—an innovatory book on using literature for language practice. Teenagers and adults. (ISBN 0 19 437094 1)

Music and Song, by Tim Murphey—'tuning in' to students' musical tastes can increase motivation and tap a rich vein of resources. All ages. (ISBN 0 19 437055 0)

Newspapers, by Peter Grundy—original ideas for making effective use of newspapers in lessons. Teenagers and adults. (ISBN 0 19 437192 6)

Projects with Young Learners, by Diane Phillips, Sarah Burwood, and Helen Dunford—encourages learner independence by producing a real sense of achievement. Age 5 to 13. (ISBN 0 19 437221 9)

Pronunciation, by Clement Laroy—imaginative activities to build confidence and improve all aspects of pronunciation. All ages. (ISBN 0 19 437087 9)

Role Play, by Gillian Porter Ladousse—controlled conversations to improvised drama, simple dialogues to complex scenarios. Teenagers and adults. (ISBN 0 19 437095 X)

Self-Access, by Susan Sheerin—advice on setting up and managing self-access study facilities, plus materials. Teenagers and adults. (ISBN 0 19 437099 2)

Storytelling with Children, by Andrew Wright—hundreds of exciting ideas for using stories to teach English to children aged 7 to 14. (ISBN 0 19 437202 2)

Translation, by Alan Duff—a wide variety of translation activities from many different subject areas. Teenagers and adults. (ISBN 0 19 437104 2)

Very Young Learners, by Vanessa Reilly and Sheila M. Ward—advice and ideas for teaching children aged 3 to 6 years, including games, songs, drama, stories, and art and crafts. (ISBN 0 19 437209 X)

Video, by Richard Cooper, Mike Lavery, and Mario Rinvolucri—original ideas for watching and making videos. All ages. (ISBN 0 19 437102 6)

Vocabulary, by John Morgan and Mario Rinvolucri—a wide variety of communicative activities for teaching new words. Teenagers and adults. (ISBN 019 437091 7)

Writing, by Tricia Hedge—a wide range of writing tasks, as well as guidance on student difficulties with writing. Teenagers and adults. (ISBN 0 19 437098 4)

Young Learners, by Sarah Phillips—advice and ideas for teaching English to children aged 6–12, including arts and crafts, games, stories, poems, and songs. (ISBN 0 19 437195 6)

Index

Note: page numbers are in *italics*. The majority of references are to project numbers.